NEW FOUNDATIONS

FOR

INSURANCE LAW

AUSTRALIA AND NEW ZEALAND
The Law Book Company Ltd.,
Sydney: Melbourne: Perth

CANADA AND U.S.A.
The Carswell Company Ltd.
Agincourt, Ontario

INDIA
N.M. Tripathi Private Ltd.
Bombay
and
Eastern Law House Private Ltd.
Calcutta and Delhi
M.P.P. House
Bangalore

ISRAEL
Steimatzky's Agency Ltd.
Jerusalem: Tel-Aviv: Haifa

MALAYSIA: SINGAPORE: BRUNEI
Malayan Law Journal (Pte.) Ltd.
Singapore and Kuala Lumpur

PAKISTAN
Pakistan Law House
Karachi

NEW FOUNDATIONS

FOR

INSURANCE LAW

CURRENT LEGAL PROBLEMS

Edited by

F. D. Rose M.A., B.C.L., Ph.D.
of Gray's Inn, Barrister,
Senior Lecturer in Laws,
University College London

London
Stevens & Sons
1987

Published in 1987
by Stevens & Sons Ltd.
of 11, New Fetter Lane, London.
Computerset by Promenade Graphics Limited, Cheltenham.
Printed in Great Britain by
Page Brothers (Norwich) Ltd.

British Library Cataloguing in Publication Data

New Foundations for Insurance Law.—(Current
Legal Problems)
1. Insurance Law—England
I. Rose, F.D.   II. Series
344.206'86   KD1859

ISBN 0–420–47780–2

©
Stevens & Sons
1987

INTRODUCTION

In addition to an annual collection of papers on a selection of different legal topics, the 40th volume of which is published this year, *Current Legal Problems* has fostered a series of specialist issues devoted to particular areas of interest, of which this volume is the fourth. Like the first and the third in this series, on taxation and company law respectively, it examines an important area of commercial law.

The complexity and fascination of commercial law owe much to its eclectic, catholic and amorphous nature and to the necessary accommodation of a variety of legal and practical considerations. With a number of important recent developments, this is increasingly true of insurance law.

In particular, this is an especially opportune moment to consider the extent to which the relationship between the parties to insurance contracts has become affected by public interest considerations. As John Birds points out, ten years ago, insurance contracts escaped the general statutory control introduced by the Unfair Contract Terms Act 1977. In return, however, the industry has been persuaded to regularise its practices in exercising its strict contractual rights by adopting Statements of Insurance Practice, both generally and in relation to long-term life insurance. Their scope is limited, in that they neither apply to all insurers nor benefit the assured where strict legal rights need to be enforced, as on insolvency. But their practical effect is widespread. They also fulfil a not insignificant legislative function: thus, they embrace Law Commission proposals so far unimplemented by Parliament. The Statements have just been revised, as has the Code of Practice for general insurance intermediaries. A proper understanding of these non-statutory schemes, and of the precise impact of the arbitration and conciliation services which have recently been established by the industry, are essential for a proper appreciation of the contemporary working of insurance business.

The self-regulatory system just described must now co-exist with the scheme of the freshly enacted Financial Services Act 1986 in the case of life assurance. The statute introduces a novel form of regulation by formally vesting in the Secretary of State for Trade and Industry rule-making powers of statutory force, together with authorisation, recognition, monitoring and enforcement roles, but providing for their delegation to a practitioner-based "private" regulatory body which will be subject to public law control and remedies. Joanna Gray discusses this possibly "most significant challenge for public law over the next few years" and the effect of the Act on insurance intermediaries, for whom there is a requirement of "polarisation," as either fully independent intermediaries or as company representatives. A particularly important feature of the new scheme is its methods of correcting the intermediary's bias towards insurers, from whom he receives his commission, and the information asymmetry between intermediary and investor. The real impact of the new scheme will only become clear with time but an appreciation of its implications and possible direction is facilitated by its examination in its economic and market context.

The more familiar private law elements of insurance law have also been subject to recent fundamental judicial development. Focusing on the landmark decision of *Banque Keyser Ullman S.A.* v. *Skandia (U.K.) Insurance Ltd.* [1987] 1 Lloyd's Rep.69, Paul Matthews considers the central doctrine of *uberrima fides*. A significant feature of current adjudication and legal writing is a broader analysis of the law and its implications from the interconnected standpoints of established precedent, legal theory and practice. Although the *uberrima fides* requirement has traditionally been perceived as applying to the assured, it is demonstrably equally relevant in principle to the obligations of the insurer. In practice, the circumstances in which insurers will be held liable, *e.g.* for non-disclosure and damages, may not be extensive; but recognition of the possibility of such liability is a vital factor to be considered in the conduct of insurance business and in the increasingly flourishing area of professional liability.

The growing attention contemporarily paid to the international aspects of commercial law in general and to contracts of reinsurance in particular is reflected in a number of important judgments discussed by Robert Merkin. Determination of the proper law of the contract in a case involving foreign elements is a process of perennial general importance both procedurally, in establishing jurisdiction over the disputants, and substantively, in deciding which law is to govern the dispute. It has attracted a good deal of attention of late specifically in relation to insurance arrangements. Not only may there be a multiplicity of parties and subject-matters with differing characteristics, especially in shipping cases, but the practice of insuring and then reinsuring on the international market has amplified the conflict of laws problems. An important consideration is the extent to which harmonisation of insurance and reinsurance cover is to be achieved through the proper law, an ideal which the cases show to be a possible, but not inevitable, consequence of incorporating express choice of law clauses.

The peculiarities of the specialised area of marine insurance are prominent in Peter Muchlinski's treatment of causation and proof of loss, major factors in the resolution of all insurance claims, whether marine or non-marine. The issues are complex and demand a careful exploration of the construction of different contractual clauses, the relationship between insured perils and excepted perils, the different causal connections between the facts, and the process of proof. Though there is a customary reservation about the mutual applicability of the rules governing marine and non-marine insurance, each area clearly derives much of importance from the other and even considerations of consumer protection, commonly regarded in relation to non-marine insurance, are seen to have their place in the maritime area.

Although the law and practice of insurance are in one sense primarily the interest of those directly involved in the business, the subject is of concern to all those affected by it—which, in one way or another, excludes no-one. The papers illustrate the extent to which there has been recent activity both in the regulation of the industry and in reconsidering the principles and rules of the law governing it. In both spheres, this activity has exhibited elements which are both continuing and innovative, whichever way the bias may lie. In some cases, significant developments are still anticipated. In all cases, it is hoped that the discussion offered here will usefully contribute to the progressive and beneficial development of this important branch of commerial law.

University College London   Francis Rose
May Day, 1987

CONTENTS

ix

TABLE OF CASES

TABLE OF STATUTES

Self-regulation and Insurance Contracts

JOHN BIRDS

A. *Introduction*

The insurance contract is, if not unique, at least unusual among contracts governed by English law in that it has survived any statutory controls of the sort imposed by the law on many other sorts of contract, for example contracts of sale[1] and contracts of hire purchase and similar credit devices.[2] This is so, notwithstanding the fact that insurance is a commodity regularly purchased, like goods, by individual consumers. The casual observer might surmise that this is because the common law of insurance does not contain doctrines which can operate harshly on the individual consumer, that there are no devices similar to, for example, the harsh exclusion clause which could deny a buyer of goods any remedy if the goods proved unsatisfactory. He would, of course, be wrong. The law of insurance contains a number of doctrines which can, in theory, operate against the interests of the innocent insured person. The potential abuses relate particularly to the wide-ranging pre-contractual duty on an insured to disclose material facts and to the fact that almost anything can be made a fundamental term of an insurance contract, even an immaterial item on a proposal form. They have been well-documented elsewhere,[3] and reference to them will be made below.

The curious thing, at first sight, is that the legislature has not stepped in to regulate these abuses. This is not for want of official reports recognising the need for interference.[4] What has happened is that the insurance industry has managed to persuade the Government that self-regulation is all that is needed. It is the purpose of this paper to examine the current state of self-regulation in the insurance area. The term "regulation" will be interpreted broadly to cover not just the Statements of Insurance Practice which are directed at traditional contractual doctrines and the codes of practice regulating the activities of insurance salesmen and other intermediaries, but also the activities of the conciliation and arbitration services which are now well-established in the insurance area. Taken together, these self-regulatory mechanisms illustrate how much the law in action differs from the law in the books, at least in the area of many insurance transactions involving individuals.

1

B. *The Statements of Insurance Practice*

One writer[5] has recently described in detail how many aspects of insurance law operate in practice pursuant to agreements made by the insurance industry, either with Government or internally. Two of these "agreements," of considerable importance to the average insurance consumer, are pronouncements by the industry, promulgated at the behest or with the consent of Government, as to the extent to which it will take advantage of traditional doctrines of non-disclosure, warranties and conditions. One relates to general insurance business (hereinafter referred to as the "General Statement"), the other to long-term (*i.e.* life) insurance (hereafter referred to as the "Long-term Statement").[6] The Statements of Insurance Practice were first made in 1977, when the insurance industry succeeded in its lobby to have contracts of insurance exempted from the Unfair Contract Terms Act. The present writer examined the original Statement of General Insurance Practice at the time.[7]

The Statements have recently been revised in some significant ways, so that in substance they now amount to a non-legislative enactment of recommendations of the Law Commission. While there is no doubt that the result is considerably better than the original Statements, the use of this method of "law reform" can, it is suggested, be convincingly criticised. First, it is a curious reflection of our Parliamentary procedures in respect of matters of law reform that time could not be found to implement what is clearly regarded on all sides as necessary reform.[8] Secondly, there is no guarantee that the Statements will be regarded as binding by all those insurers involved in selling to individuals. Although this would no doubt in practice involve only a minority of insurers, the fact that there are insurers outside the traditional trade associations, the Association of British Insurers and Lloyd's of London, should surely have persuaded the Government that self-regulation was not enough.[9]

Space forbids amplification of these criticisms. It is perhaps more important, given that time for insurance law reform is unlikely to be found for the foreseeable future, to examine the history and terms of the Statements. As already mentioned, as revised they reflect recommendations made by the Law Commission in 1980.[10] Although the insurance industry lobbied hard against the Commission's report, the fact that the report found favour with the Government[11] meant that the industry was obliged to go along with it to some extent. Its greatest success was to persuade the Department of Trade and Industry that any reform should be limited to insurance contracts entered into by private individuals. While this may not be unduly hard on the large commercial undertaking, armed with professional advisers, it does seem potentially harsh on the small business insured. For some time the Department was clearly minded to introduce legislation; indeed, at one time it acceded to persuasive arguments made by the consumer lobby that the Law Commission had not gone far enough and was on the point of drafting a Bill which would have in effect abolished the doctrine of *uberrima fides* altogether in the private insurance context. Apparently, however, the drafting of the Bill proved too difficult. It then transpired that Parliamentary time was taken up with other things, and in February 1986, the revision of the Statements was announced instead.[12]

1. *Non-disclosure and misrepresentation*

It is in respect of the doctrines of non-disclosure and misrepresentation that the Statements have most effect on the common law of insurance. These are covered rather curiously under the heading "Claims," perhaps because it is in practice only when a claim is made that an insurer will avoid on these grounds. In effect innocent non-disclosure or misrepresentation are made not actionable. Paragraph 2(b) of the General Statement provides:

> "An insurer will not repudiate liability to indemnify a policy-holder:—
> (i) on grounds of non-disclosure of a material fact which a policyholder could not reasonably be expected to have disclosed;
> (ii) on grounds of misrepresentation unless it is a deliberate or negligent misrepresentation of a material fact."

The Long-term Statement, para. 3(a) makes similar provision in a strangely different way:

> "An insurer will not unreasonably reject a claim. In particular, an insurer will not reject a claim or invalidate a policy on grounds of non-disclosure or misrepresentation of a fact unless:
> (i) it is a material fact; and
> (ii) it is a fact within the knowledge of the proposer; and
> (iii) it is a fact which the proposer could reasonably be expected to disclose.
> (It should be noted that fraud or deception will, and reckless or negligent non-disclosure or misrepresentation of a material fact may, constitute grounds for rejection of a claim.)"

These provisions must be read in conjunction with the requirements of both Statements that proposers must be warned on proposal forms and, in respect of general insurance, on renewal notices, of the need for disclosure. These requirements as to warnings are discussed below. It should be noted that the standard of reasonableness by which a non-disclosure or misrepresentation is to be judged appears to be that of the actual proposer in question and that, therefore, what a reasonable proposer would have done is not conclusive. Presumably, though, the proposer must be expected to have read the warnings about the need for proper disclosure and, where the intermediaries' code of conduct (which is considered later in this paper) applies, he should have been fully alerted to what is necessary. Conversely, insurers are expected to ask clear questions about facts which have generally been found to be material,[13] and to refrain from asking questions requiring expert knowledge to answer them.[14] It is interesting to note that, in a non-disclosure case where a warning of the above sort had been included on the insurer's proposal form,[15] the judge seemed to interpret the warning as a waiver of the insured's duty of disclosure of matters outside the questions expressly asked on the form, though this decision can be criticised as going beyond the traditional application of the doctrine of waiver.[16]

The extract cited above from the Long-term Statement is badly worded. The first sentence is an undesirable hangover from the original Statement since it seems to allow an insurer to reject a claim when *it* thinks it reasonable to do so (this was an undesirable feature of the original General Statement, but the phrase no longer appears there). Sub-paragraph (i) is curious, given that the law requires that a fact has to be material before non-disclosure or misrepresentation of it can be relied upon. The sentence in parenthesis is odd (it is also, incidentally, carried forward from the original Statement). Why does it include a reference to negligence when this seems to have been covered by (iii)? The implication of the extract without the sentence in brackets is that negligent non-disclosure or misrepresentation will entitle an insurer to repudiate; the parenthesis then says that this "may" constitute grounds for rejection. This is unnecessary ambiguity. It is perhaps a pity that the life offices could not have been persuaded to provide for a misrepresentation of age alone in a proposal form by allowing a proportionate recovery calculated by reference to the true, as opposed to the mis-stated, age of the proposer at the time of the proposal. It may be that in practice they do operate in this way, but a formal statement to that effect would have been useful.[17]

2. *Warranties and conditions*

In insurance contract law, the warranty is closely linked in theory with the duty of disclosure, since it was standard practice, by means of a "basis of the contract clause," to convert statements made on an insurance proposal form into warranties, that is, fundamental terms of the contract breach of which would entitle the insurer to treat the subsequent contract as repudiated.[18] This is not to deny that warranties could not, and cannot, be found in the body of the insurance policy itself, although frequently in practice such terms may be called conditions precedent.[19] The Law Commission[20] called for the formal abolition of the basis of the contract clause in respect of statements as to past or present facts on a proposal form; and in respect of individual insurances this is in effect done by the General Statement, which requires completion of the proposal form to be to the best of the proposer's knowledge and belief only,[21] and provides that neither the form nor the policy should contain any provision converting the statements in the form as to past or present facts into warranties.[22] Paragraph 1(b) of the Long-term Statement contains provision to the same effect as the latter provision in the General Statement.

It should be noted that paragraph 1(b) in both Statements contains what seems to be a saving provision allowing insurers to require specific warranties about matters that are material to the risk. This hardly seems necessary given that no one would surely deny the right of insurers to have terms such as those regarding precautions which the insured must take to safeguard the risk insured against. What is needed is provision to ensure that breach of such terms is not repudiatory unless the consequences justify it. The Law Commission dealt with this point by requiring a causal connection between a breach of warranty and a loss before the insurer could deny liability to pay for the loss.[23] The General Statement follows this to some extent,[24] although with an exception where "fraud is involved." This exception is unfortunate. Why should an insurer not have to prove a suspected fraudulent claim, instead of being able to rely on what may well be a fortuitous unconnected breach of warranty or condition?

It is also unclear whether the restriction on repudiation—"where the circumstances of the loss are unconnected with the breach [of warranty or condition]"—is as sophisticated as the Law Commission recommended. It clearly covers the sort of case where, for example, a motor insured has broken a warranty requiring him to maintain his vehicle in a roadworthy condition and the loss is a wholly unconnected theft. It is not clear that it covers the case (where the Law Commission thought the insured should also be protected) where, using the same example, the loss occurs in an accident, so that there is a prima facie connection, but the insured can prove on the facts that his failure to maintain did not contribute to the accident.

3. *Warnings and statements*

The original Statements contained requirements as to warnings and statements which should be included by insurers on their documents. These requirements are extended by the revised Statements. There is an important point of principle here since many of the warnings relate to the duty of disclosure and it can perhaps be argued that retention of the duty, at least in individual insurances, can be justified only if proposers and policyholders are aware of its existence. Certainly, one of the most persuasive arguments against the whole notion of *uberrima fides* is the fact that the vast majority of people must be unaware of its existence, let alone what it implies. A survey conducted after the original Statements had been in force for some time found that many of these warnings were not displayed in a way which would mean anything to the average insurance consumer reading his proposal form or renewal notice.[25] The industry has responded to this in part by requiring that the warnings and statements required on proposal forms are *prominent*. These are as follows in respect of the General Statement:

1. A statement "(i) drawing the attention of the proposer to the consequences of the failure to disclose material facts, explained as those facts an insurer would regard as likely to influence the acceptance and assessment of the proposal; (ii) warning that if the proposer is in any doubt about facts considered material, he should disclose them."[26] The importance of this is obvious from what has already been said above, though it must be noted that a prominent statement to this effect is required only if the statement is not included in the declaration at the foot of the proposal form. If the latter is the case, prominence is not, it seems, required.

2. A statement that a specimen policy form is available unless the prospectus or proposal form contains full details.[27]

3. A warning to the proposer to keep a record of all information he has supplied to the insurer.[28]

4. A statement that a copy of the completed form is automatically provided for retention at the time of completion, or will be supplied as part of the insurer's normal practice, or will be supplied on request within a period of three months after its com-

pletion.[29] What in effect thus imposes an obligation on insurers to keep proposal forms accessible to policyholders, which is important given that they are usually part of the contract between the parties and which is in keeping with the spirit of a recommendation of the Law Commission,[30] is reinforced by paragraph 1(h), which provides that an insurer will not raise an issue under a proposal form unless the policyholder is provided with a copy of it as completed.

All these statements and warnings are to be welcomed. What must be ensured is that the prominence required is really adhered to by the industry in a meaningful way.

By contrast, the two warnings required by paragraph 3 of the General Statement to be included on renewal notices are not required to be prominent. These warnings relate to the duty of disclosure on renewal, including in respect of changes affecting the policy, and to the keeping of records by the insured of all information supplied to the insurer. It is this writer's experience that the warning as to disclosure, which has been required since the original Statement, is often not made by insurers in a way which makes clear to the average consumer the importance of disclosure. It is surprising, therefore, that the requirement of prominence does not appear here. It seems self-evident that the average proposer for insurance realises the importance of disclosing at least some information to the insurer, given that the insurer solicits a great deal of information by means of express questions on a proposal form. It is certainly not so clear that the average insured realises the need for disclosure on renewal, as no questions are expressly put to him. All he is probably concerned with is the amount of renewal premium required. It is to be hoped that insurers go beyond the letter of the Statement in this respect and improve renewal notice warnings in such a way as to make it absolutely clear what the law and practice requires of the renewer in this respect. It might even help if there were a separate sheet included with the letter inviting renewal, headed "Disclosure." This could contain the warning and, for the insured with anything to disclose, space to put it down.[31]

4. *Miscellaneous*

There are other provisions of the Statements, most of which will not be considered here. Attention, though, is drawn to two points. First, the provisions of the Statements are binding on the Insurance Ombudsman and any arbitrator appointed under the Personal Insurance Arbitration Services (P.I.A.S.) system.[32]

Secondly, insurers undertake to develop clearer and more explicit proposal forms and policy documents "whilst bearing in mind the legal nature of insurance contracts."[33] This acceptance of the desirability of "plain English," which some insurers have been concerned to adopt for several years now, is welcome, although it must not be forgotten that plain English is not a cure for all potential difficulties of interpretation of words, as the Insurance Ombudsman has recently pointed out.[34]

C. *Codes of Practice for Intermediaries*

The importance of the need for independent and competent intermediaries in the insurance area was stressed by a Consumer Council study in 1970.[35] Apart from fairly limited statutory intervention,[36] it was not until 1980 that legislation in the form of the Insurance Brokers (Registration) Act 1977 was implemented. That Act, and the regulations made under it, has established a model form of self-regulation under statutory authority.[37] The Act has been amended by section 138 of the Financial Services Act 1986 so as to ensure compatability between it and the regulatory system for the selling of investments (including life insurance) established under the 1986 Act.[38]

As far as non-broker intermediaries are concerned, there is no statutory regulation other than the limited sort mentioned above.[39] Instead, codes of conduct have been issued (originally in 1981) by what is now the Association of British Insurers (A.B.I.), and member companies are obliged to ensure that the codes are observed. These are thus another example of self-regulation in the insurance field without statutory backing, but again it must be observed that a minority of insurers, and hence of intermediaries, is not subject to it.

There are two codes. The *Life Assurance Selling—Code of Practice* is the more detailed, which is not surprising, given the complexity of most modern life assurance schemes. This code will be superseded by conduct of business rules to be made under the framework of the Financial Services Act 1986. Of more immediate interest is the *General Insurance Business—Code of Practice for all Intermediaries (Including Employees of Insurance Companies) other than Registered Insurance Brokers*, which the A.B.I. has recently reviewed.[40] This will survive (as amended) because the 1986 Act is not, with limited exceptions,[41] concerned with general insurance business. While this must be right, there may come a time when statutory authority becomes necessary, because of the non-comprehensive coverage of the code mentioned above.[42] In the meantime, the code can be used as evidence of the standards of care and skill expected of insurance intermediaries. This is not unimportant given the increasing number of legal actions pursued against intermediaries.[43] As mentioned above, the code has recently been reviewed and is likely to be amended in the very near future. This account will consider the original code and then examine the likely revisions.[44]

1. *The original code*

Apart from stating the general principle that it is an overriding obligation of an intermediary at all times to conduct business with the utmost good faith and integrity, the code falls into two parts. Part II can be dealt with quite quickly. It is concerned with when an intermediary is acting solely as an introducer and attempts to ensure that he does no more than that, obliging him to give advice only on those matters in which he is competent and to transmit enquiries at the earliest opportunity to the insurer. He is forbidden to go outside the terms of his agency appointment and to influence the prospective policyholder with regard to the completion of the proposal form.

Part I applies to the selling and servicing of general insurance policies and thus applies particularly to agents of insurers with authority so to act and to intermediaries who are not registered insurance brokers, that is, insurance consultants and the like. There is some detailed control over selling. Cold-calling is not prohibited provided that it is at a time likely to be suitable to the prospective policyholder, although "where appropriate," the intermediary should make a prior appointment. This seems excessively vague and it could be argued that all cold-calling should be banned.[45] The intermediary must identify what he is about as soon as possible, ensure that any insurance proposed is suitable for the proposer, give advice only in respect of matters in which he is knowledgeable, and observe confidentiality. He must not make inaccurate or unfair criticisms of any insurer nor make comparisons with other types of policies without making clear the differing characteristics of each policy. Furthermore, he must not disclose that the name of the prospective policyholder was given by another unless he is prepared to disclose the latter's name and has the latter's consent to do so. The above provisions impose duties some of which may be said to be of a quasi-fiduciary nature. There are provisions of a similar nature regarding the keeping of accounts and the treatment of money received.

Of direct relevance to the question of the standards of skill and care expected are the provisions regarding "Explanation of the

Contract" and "Disclosure of Underwriting Information." Among other things, the intermediary is expected to explain all the essential provisions of the policy he is recommending so as to ensure so far as possible that the prospective policyholder understands what he is buying and to draw attention to any restrictions and exclusions applying to the policy. This seems like a potentially onerous duty given the complicated technical nature of most insurance contracts, even those worded in "plain English," and one may wonder how often it is really complied with.

The provisions relating to the proposal form reflect the legal position and the Statements of Practice discussed earlier. The intermediary must avoid influencing the proposer and must make it clear that all the answers or statements are the latter's responsibility, and he must ensure that the consequences of non-disclosure and inaccuracies are pointed out to the proposer by drawing his attention to the relevant statement in the proposal form, that is the one required by the Statement of Practice,[46] and by explaining them himself to the proposer. As far as concerns the answering of questions etc. on the form, one can only express the hope that the code is observed. It is, however, interesting, and perhaps unfortunate, that the code does not actually require that the proposer himself fill in the answers. If it did, then perhaps the scenario evident in the well-known line of cases which, perhaps unfortunately, attributes an agent's misdeeds to even an innocent proposer[47] would be unlikely to arise. As it is, if the agent does still fill in the form,[48] it may be suspected that many proposers will not actually thoroughly check it through, no matter how much it is suggested that they do so. As far as disclosure is concerned, observance of the code should in theory ensure that the average proposer is aware of the duty to disclose and what it means. Again, one hopes that this is what happens.

2. *The revisions to the code*

The proposed revisions to the code have been influenced by the conduct of business rules to be made under the auspices of the Financial Services Act 1986. Perhaps the most important change is the requirement that the intermediary specify at the outset his exact status and who, if anyone, bears responsibility for his actions. Thus, he must disclose whether he is an employee of an insurance company for whom the company is liable, an agent representing one or more companies for whom the latter are liable, or an independent intermediary (that is, one not registered as a broker) for whom no insurer will accept responsibility. In line with this, the A.B.I. proposes to require the adoption by its member companies of standard criteria for the appointment of intermediaries.[49]

In addition, the terms of the code have to be incorporated verbatim or by reference in all Letters of Appointment of non-registered intermediaries as agents of the company and no policy may be sold by such agents except within the terms of such an agency agreement.

Perhaps the only notable omission from the code as revised is the lack of any provision requiring an intermediary to disclose the commission he would receive. Such disclosure is required by the life assurance code and will be required under the conduct of business rules which will replace that code. This omission is regrettable since the level of commission must surely influence particularly the non-registered independent intermediary in relation to which insurer he recommends.

3. Conclusion

In concluding this part of this paper, it is perhaps appropriate to stress the links between the intermediaries' code of conduct and the Statement of Practice discussed earlier. In respect of the duty of disclosure etc., they should together ensure that the law is operated fairly in respect of many individual insurance consumers. The policyholder who deals through an intermediary is in a much better position to understand the full implications of an insurance transaction than someone who deals directly with an insurance company. Furthermore, if the intermediary fails to do his job properly, then the policyholder may have a legal remedy against him which by definition is not available to someone who does not use an intermediary's services, or, if the intermediary is actually employed by the insurer, may be able in law to attribute liability to the insurer for the acts of its agent.

D. *Arbitration and Concilation Services*

It seems to have been as a response to increasing concern among consumer representatives about insurance contract law that three of the biggest United Kingdom insurers established the Insurance Ombudsman Bureau (I.O.B.) in March 1981.[50] The I.O.B. was not welcomed by the whole industry, possibly because it was feared that the Ombudsman would be a consumer champion, and a rival organisation, Personal Insurance Arbitration Services (P.I.A.S.), was set up in the following year. The I.O.B. quickly established the dominant position, and now companies insuring over 70 per cent. of personal policyholders belong. P.I.A.S. still exists, however, and one large group belongs to both organisations. The reason why the I.O.B. proved so successful so quickly is probably because experience soon showed that the Ombudsman was not by any means a consumer champion, but a genuinely independent conciliator and arbitrator. In any event, the I.O.B. was identified outside the industry as an excellent model to be followed[51]; it has already been followed by the establishment of the Banking Ombudsman, and other service industries are expected to follow suit, especially as a result of the self-regulatory mechanisms being established under the Financial Services Act 1986. The remainder of this paper will briefly review the functions of the I.O.B. and P.I.A.S.

1. The Insurance Ombudsman Bureau

The Bureau itself is an unlimited company with a board of directors appointed as representatives of the member companies. It has an independent Council, the majority of whose members are not industry people, and it is the Council which appoints and oversees the Ombudsman. Like the Statements of Practice, the Ombudsman has jurisdiction over personal insurances only. His services are free to policyholders and he can make awards binding on the insurer concerned of up to £100,000.[52] The insured, though, is not bound by his decisions and is free to take legal action if dissatisfied.[53] A case reaches the Ombudsman's jurisdiction only when all the internal procedures of the insurer concerned, up to chief executive level, have been exhausted.[54]

Very rarely indeed does the Ombudsman actually exercise his power to make a formal arbitral award. His decisions are usually accepted in a much less formal way. Throughout the period of his existence, the Ombudsman has been concerned to stress the importance of this his conciliatory role and of his impartiality. He does not see himself as a representative of one side or the other. This point has been regularly made in his annual reports, which make fascinating reading for those with an interest in the area. Apart from describing his *modus operandi* and giving regular advice to insurers and policyholders alike, these reports give summaries of the more important of the Ombudsman's decisions during the year. It is always stressed, however, that, while he favours

consistency, the Ombudsman does not regard his decisions as lay-
ing down precedents to be slavishly followed in the future.[55] He
regards the discretion he has under the terms of his authority as
all-important, a point which is mentioned again below.

The years have seen a substantial increase in the number of
complaints referred to the Ombudsman, something which is not
accounted for simply by the increase in the number of member
companies.[56] No doubt, increasing awareness of his existence has
also been a factor.[57] However, it must never be forgotten that the
number of complaints is but a tiny proportion of the number of
claims made on insurers who are members of the I.O.B.

The fact that the Ombudsman sees himself as a conciliator as
much as an arbitrator has already been mentioned. This ties in
with the way he works. In his very first report,[58] the Ombudsman
described this. Sometimes he is called on to resolve issues of fact,
perhaps where there has been a misunderstanding over a claim.
Other complaints turn on disputes as to the law, particularly over
the interpretation of policy wordings. In this respect, he regularly
seeks and relies on expert advice, as well as, of course, where relevant, on case-law. However, the overall and most crucial point is
the fact that he has discretion. He is not bound to follow the law
and certainly would not do so where good insurance practice dic-
tated otherwise. This is especially so in respect of the questions of
non-disclosure, etc. which are governed by the Statements of Practice discussed earlier. Indeed, as already mentioned, the terms of
the Statements are binding on the Ombudsman.[59]

As often as not, the Ombudsman ends up supporting the
insurer's decision, although he has given much sound and quite
stern advice to insurers, especially concerning the wording of their
proposal forms and policies. He often takes a traditional contract
lawyer's view of things, particularly in his stressing that it is the
proposer's responsibility to check the accuracy of a proposal form,
even when it is completed by an intermediary, and in his interpretation of standard-form terms such as warranties imposing on the
insured a duty to take reasonable care of insured property or
reasonable care to avoid a loss.[60] Overall, however, there seems
little doubt that the institution is a very successful and useful one.
As in respect of the Statements and Codes discussed earlier in this
paper, one can only regret that there remains a substantial minority of insurers outside the institution. Perhaps in time this will
change. It could be provided that membership of the Bureau be a
condition of authorisation to conduct personal insurance business,
something which would be in line with the current framework of
self-regulation under the Financial Services Act 1986.

2. *Personal Insurances Arbitration Service*

P.I.A.S. is quite different from the I.O.B. in a number of ways. In particular, it is an arbitration service in the traditional sense that the decision of the arbitrator is binding on both parties. There is no formal organisation like the I.O.B. The member companies have simply agreed that, in the event of a dispute, their policyholders should have the right to take the claim to an arbitrator appointed by the Chartered Institute of Arbitrators. Like the Ombudsman, however, the arbitrator's services are free to the policyholder and he will take account of the Statements of Practice as well as the law.

The real difficulty with P.I.A.S. is that there is no published information about its workings. Thus, it is impossible to know how often it is used and with what results. No doubt, the disputes are very similar to those presented to the Ombudsman, but it seems unlikely that an arbitrator has the same discretion as is vested in the Ombudsman. The future of P.I.A.S. looks to be uncertain. In respect of investment insurance—that is, most forms of life insurance, which will be governed by the Financial Services Act 1986—the need to ensure proper complaint-solving mechanisms which are universally applicable will almost certainly drive all life companies into the arms of the I.O.B. As far as general insurance is concerned, it may be that P.I.A.S. will continue to exist in a small number of cases. It is surely to be hoped, though,[61] that it will merge with the I.O.B. in the near future.

E. *Conclusion*

The review in this paper of what are thought to be the principal self-regulatory devices in the area of personal insurance contract law must conclude by pointing out the provisional and largely unscientific nature of many of the comments made herein. In assessing these devices, it is necessary to make *a priori* judgments because there is no real empirical evidence, or at least published evidence, as to how they work. The Ombudsman says that he works well, the Department of Trade and Industry and the Association of British Insurers are both on record at various times as stating how self-regulation has worked satisfactorily, but no one has yet, it seems, been permitted to go behind these public declarations and actually examine complaints files or claims files or talk to aggrieved policyholders. Such evidence as there is is often anecdotal. It is certainly not statistically valid. If access to the various sources were ever permitted, there would be much useful work to be done in this area.

Notes

[1] See the Sale of Goods Act 1979 and, in particular, the controls on exclusion clauses in the Unfair Contract Terms Act 1977.

[2] See the Consumer Credit Act 1974 and the regulations made thereunder.

[3] See in particular the influential articles by Hasson, "The doctrine of uberrima fides in insurance law—a critical evaluation" (1969) 32 M.L.R. 615 and "The basis of the contract clause in insurance law" (1971) 34 M.L.R. 29; the 5th Report of the Law Reform Committee, *Conditions and exceptions in insurance policies*, Cmnd. 62 (1957); the Law Commission's Report No. 104, *Insurance Law—Non-disclosure and breach of warranty*, Cmnd. 8064 (1980); and see for a survey, Birds, *Modern Insurance Law* (1982), at pp. 99–104 and 118–120. For consideration of recent developments regarding the duty of disclosure, see Matthews, "Uberrima Fides in Modern Insurance Law," *post*, Chap. 3. It must not be forgotten that many reputable insurers have for many years not sought to rely on their strict legal rights. In practice this would be unlikely anyway, since, for example, the range of material facts which the law theoretically requires a proposer for (and a renewer of) an insurance contract to disclose would mean that hardly any insured was not guilty of some non-disclosure. Where the so called "technical defences" were and, perhaps, are used is in cases of suspected but unprovable fraud: see the Law Reform Committee Report, *op. cit.*, para. 11. As the Law Commission pointed out (*op. cit.*, para. 3.27), this is not really morally justifiable.

[4] See in particular those referred to in the previous footnote, and note that the reference to the Law Commission was due to the presence of a proposed E.E.C. Directive rather than to particular internal pressure for reform. Reform agencies in other common law jurisdictions have recommended reform: see, in particular, the Australian Law Reform Committee's important Report No. 20 on *Insurance Contracts* (1982), which resulted very quickly in comprehensive legislation (the Insurance Contracts Act 1984).

[5] Lewis, "Insurers' agreements not to enforce strict legal rights: bargaining with government and in the shadow of the law" (1985) 48 M.L.R. 275.

[6] The text of the Statements can be found in Part 7 of the *Encyclopedia of Insurance Law* (Sweet & Maxwell) and in (1986) 83 *Law Society Gazette* 2338–2340.

[7] See Birds (1977) 40 M.L.R. 677. Although it is clear that the Law Commission when recommending what became the Unfair Contract Terms Act intended insurance contracts to be within its scope, it is not certain what effect the application of the Act, especially s.3, would have had in the area of insurance. Arguably, it would have been inappropriate to cover the duty of disclosure and related doctrines, the operation of which has long been recognised as potentially the harshest in insurance law.

[8] For a damning comment on the Department of Trade and Industry's failure to implement the Law Commission's Report, see North, "Law reform: processes and problems" (1985) 101 L.Q.R. 338 at pp. 349–350.

[9] The D.T.I. "expects" this minority of insurers to comply. In the words of the Secretary of State (H.C.Debs. February 21, 1986, col. 358): "I look to all insurers, whether or not they belong to the Association of British Insurers, to observe both their spirit and their letter." *Quaere* whether this is enough. The problem is that proper information on insurance company practices is difficult to obtain, a point made again in the conclusion to this paper. Occasionally a striking case of the use of a "technical defence" may hit the headlines, but we do not know how typical that is. There have been cases referred to the Insurance Ombudsman where an insurer has used pure non-disclosure as a defence, even when the proposal had been made after the first Statements of Practice. If this can happen in respect of a "reputable" company, it seems quite likely that it will happen in respect of insurers who are not

members of the Insurance Ombudsman Bureau and/or the Association of British Insurers. Furthermore, the liquidator of a failed insurance company would be bound to reject any claim that was legally capable of being repudiated. It must not be forgotten that the costs of administering claims means that in respect of claims below a certain figure often insurers do little more than skim through a claim form and write a cheque for the amount claimed.

[10] Law Com.No. 104 (*supra*, n. 3).

[11] See the Department of Trade memorandum of October 31, 1980 "Insurance Contract Law: the need for reform," responding to the Law Commission Report.

[12] H.C.Debs. February 21, 1986, cols. 358–359. Earlier Parliamentary statements, which provide an interesting reflection of behind the scenes lobbying and consultation, as well as illustrating how the Government's views as to the need for legislation changed quite dramatically, can be found in H.C.Debs. June 3, 1981, cols. 1029–1043, April 28, 1983, col. 376 and March 28, 1984, col. 280. For other comment on the revised Statements, see Forte (1986) 49 M.L.R. 754.

[13] General Statement, para. 1(*a*); Long-term Statement, para. 1(*c*).

[14] *Ibid.* para. 1(*e*) and 1(*d*), respectively. "Materiality" will be judged by reference to the law, as to which see in particular *Lambert* v. *Co-operative Insurance Society* [1975] 2 Lloyd's Rep. 485 and *Container Transport International Inc.* v. *Oceanus Mutual Underwriting Association (Bermuda) Ltd.* [1984] 1 Lloyd's Rep. 476.

[15] *Hair* v. *Prudential Assurance Co.* [1983] 2 Lloyd's Rep. 667.

[16] See Birds [1984] J.B.L. 163.

[17] This sort of provision can be found in other common law jurisdictions: *e.g.*, the New Zealand Insurance Law Reform Act 1977, s.7 and the Australian Insurance Contracts Act, s.30.

[18] The leading case is *Dawsons Ltd.* v. *Bonnin* [1922] 2 A.C. 413. The history of the device is traced in Hasson (1971) 34 M.L.R. 29.

[19] It is clear that the nomenclature makes no difference to the result. If a condition imposing a continuing obligation on the insured is made a fundamental term (which in practice is always likely these days), then a breach has the same effect as a breach of warranty. In practice, however, conditions will often embrace in addition less fundamental obligations, for example in relation to the claims procedure, than have traditionally been the subject of warranties. Warranties are traditionally concerned with promises or statements by the insured material to the risk insured against. It is interesting to note that fairly recently the Court of Appeal in *Cox* v. *Orion Insurance Co.* [1982] R.T.R. 1 found nothing wrong in a fairly trivial condition's being made fundamental, so that on breach the insurer had the right to treat the whole contract, and not just a particular claim, as repudiated. This decision might be thought to reflect how the law regarding insurance contracts is often way out of line with general contract law developments.

[20] Law Com.No. 104 (*supra*, n. 3), paras. 7.5–7.9.

[21] Para. 1(*a*).

[22] Para. 1(*b*).

[23] *Ibid.* para. 6.22.

[24] Para. 2(*b*)(iii). There is a more elaborate statement, to generally similar effect, in para. 3(b) of the Long-term Statement.

[25] Scottish Consumer Council, *Forms without Fuss* (March 1981).

[26] Para. 1(*c*).

[27] Para. 1(*f*).

[28] Para. 1(*g*).

[29] Para. 1(*h*).

[30] Law Com. Report No. 104, para. 4.63.

[31] A similar point was made by the Insurance Ombudsman in his Annual Report for 1983, at p. 7.

[32] Para. 6 and para. 4, of the General and the Long-term Statements, respectively. As to the Ombudsman and P.I.A.S., see *post*.

[33] Para. 5 and 2(a) of the General and the Long-term Statements, respectively.

[34] See his Annual Report for 1985, at pp. 24–25.

[35] *Study on Insurance* (1970), pp. 32–34.

[36] Regs. 67–69 of the Insurance Companies Regulations 1981 (S.I. No. 1654), made under s.74 of the Insurance Companies Act 1982 (re-enacting regulations first made in 1976).

[37] For a general description of the background, see Graham, "The Bank of England, the City and the reform of the Stock Exchange: Continuing the self-regulatory community?" (1985) 36 N.I.L.Q. 122.

[38] See further Gray, "Insurance Intermediaries and the Financial Services Act", *post*, Chap. 2.

[39] See *supra*, n. 36.

[40] Association of British Insurers, *The Selling of General Insurance* (July 1986). This document also contains a review of the 1977 Act.

[41] There are provisions concerning contracts made by unauthorised insurers (s.132) and misleading statements etc. regarding insurance contracts (s.133, replacing s.73 of the Insurance Companies Act 1982).

[42] The A.B.I. (*op. cit.*, n. 40) thinks that self-regulation is sufficient, given that the code has worked very satisfactorily. "Satisfaction" is judged according to the low number of complaints received, but presumably their review was limited to their member companies and intermediaries through which the member companies act.

[43] The number of reported decisions is comparatively large, quite apart from the likely volume of unreported, settled, cases in the County Court, etc.

[44] According to the A.B.I.'s document (*supra*, n. 40).

[45] The arguments in favour of banning cold-calling for the selling of investments are well put by Gower, although it is not suggested that they are quite so cogent in respect of non-investment insurance. See Gower, *Review of Investor Protection*, Cmnd. 9125 (1984), at paras. 8.09–8.19. In general, the rules to be made by the Securities and Investment Board under the Financial Services Act 1986 will prohibit cold-calling on individuals in respect of investments.

[46] See *ante*, p. 6.

[47] That is, the line of cases exemplified in the notorious decision of the Court of Appeal in *Newsholme Bros.* v. *Road Transport & General Insurance Co.* [1929] 2 K.B. 356. See generally, Birds, *Modern Insurance Law*, at pp. 120–125.

[48] According to the Insurance Ombudsman (Annual Report for 1985, p. 6) this is still a frequent occurrence. The Ombudsman's most regular piece of advice to policyholders in virtually all his annual reports has been to check the accuracy of the contents of the proposal form when the answers have been filled in by an intermediary of one sort or another. See *post*, n. 60.

[49] *Op. cit.* (*supra*, n. 40), Appx., Part H.

[50] There was certainly no external pressure for such a body. It is hardly mere coincidence that the date of establishment was shortly after completion of the Law Commission's Report No. 104 (*supra*, n. 3).

[51] See the National Consumer Council report, *Banking Services and the Consumer* (1983).

[52] £10,000 per annum in respect of health insurance.

[53] This factor was also influential in leading to the establishment of the rival P.I.A.S.

[54] The many queries reaching the I.O.B. before this stage are referred back.

[55] To this end, he has deprecated the citing of his decisions by member com-

panies as authority for the rejection of a claim. See the Annual Report for 1985, at p. 3, a point repeated in the Annual Report for 1986, at p. 32.

[56] Roughly a sevenfold increase in complaints as against a fourfold increase in membership.

[57] The I.O.B. also receives a great number of general insurance queries as well as complaints outside the Ombudsman's terms of reference, *e.g.* relating to intermediaries. The complainant is referred on to the appropriate trade association, *e.g.* the Association of British Insurers or the British Insurance Brokers Association.

[58] Annual Report for 1981, at pp. 10–12.

[59] See *ante*, p. 7.

[60] I have picked these points out of the six Annual Reports so far produced by the Ombudsman as seemingly the most common matters affecting policyholders to which he draws attention and as clearly two of the most common causes for the repudiation of claims, other than the defence that the loss was not actually covered by the policy. The first point, relating to an agent's completion of a proposal form is made in each of these reports; compare the comments made *ante*, in the text to nn. 47 and 48.

[61] This was the view expressed by Gower, *Review of Investor Protection*, Cmnd. 9125 (1984), para. 8.56.

Insurance Intermediaries and the Financial Services Act

JOANNA GRAY

It is difficult to assess the practical impact of any law reform whilst it is still developing its true identity and particularly difficult to do so in the case of the Financial Services Act 1986. Apart from the fact that the regulations and rules to be made under the Act are not yet in final form, the real impact of new regulation of any industry can only begin to be discerned after enough time has elapsed for a "living" regulatory pattern to emerge. This article is in a sense being written several years too early and it would be premature to try to predict now what the effects of the new regulatory scheme covering insurance intermediaries will be. What it can usefully do is to outline both the structure and content of some current proposals for the regulation of insurance intermediaries and provide some thoughts on the value of the new regulatory scheme and its ability to fulfil its stated objectives.

Scope of the Financial Services Act

The Act restricts the carrying on of investment business to persons who are either authorised to do so or exempted from its provisions. "Investment" is defined so as to include life assurance,[1] and "investment business" encompasses advice on and arranging deals in investments. Thus, those insurance brokers, agents and company employees whose activities include advising on and marketing life assurance are within the scope of the Act's scheme of regulation. The consequences of carrying on an investment business without authorisation or exemption under the Act are a criminal sanction and the unenforceability of investment agreements made in the course of that business. The Act vests formal regulatory powers in the Secretary of State for Trade and Industry, who, in turn, will delegate them to the Securities and Investments Board Ltd. (the SIB), the designated agency. This body is interesting in public law terms in that it is a practitioner-based self-financing "private" regulator with rule-making powers of statutory force and all the authorisation, recognition, monitoring and enforcement roles technically vested in the Secretary of State. This type of regulation is entirely novel in the United Kingdom and is aimed at combining the supposed (but rarely tested) advantages and disadvantages of the polar extremes of occupational self-regulation and public governmental regulation.[2] Fears about public accountability arising from the S.I.B.'s novel characteristics should be allayed by the comments of Professor Gower in the second part of his *Review of Investor Protection*, which preceded the legislation:

> " . . . despite the fact that the proposed institutional framework may be regarded as a constitutional anomaly, in that it purports to delegate public functions to a private body, it is not one which frightens me or one which, in my view, should frighten Parliament. The Board . . . will truly be practitioner-based—but so should be any Securities or Investments Commission. In form, it may be a private body . . . and, if that will ensure the maximum collaboration of City institutions, why not? The substance is that it will be exercising public functions conferred by statute and be subject to the statutory and public law constraints just as if it was a public body incorporated by statute . . . "[3]

His comments were made before the Financial Services Act had been amended to name specifically the SIB as the designated agency to which the Secretary of State's regulatory powers could be transferred. This significant mention in the Act will place the SIB more firmly within reach of public law remedies and control. Extending its principles so as to shape the way in which the SIB and the plethora of self-regulating organisations it will recognise conduct their regulatory business may well prove the single most significant challenge for public law over the next few years.[4]

One route to authorisation as an investment business under the Act will be to apply directly to the SIB for authorisation and to subject oneself to the rules promulgated by the SIB regulating investment business. These rules are to cover a wide variety of aspects of the conduct of investment business, ranging from the regulation of accounting arrangements for clients' money through to the manner in which unsolicited calls on clients should be conducted.[5] The SIB has published its draft rulebook which includes regulations relating to: authorisation as an investment business; conduct of business; unsolicited calls; cancellation of investment agreements; and clients' money. These rules are expected to form the blueprint for the rules of membership of the recognised self-regulating organisations through which membership the majority of investment businesses will gain authorisation under the Act. It is now beginning to be clear which bodies will emerge as recognised self-regulating organisations (SROs). Any body applying to the SIB for recognition must satisfy it that its members will be fit and proper persons to carry on the particular investment business with which it is concerned and that the rules to which its members are subject afford the same level of investor protection as do the rules governing the conduct of investment business promulgated by the SIB.[6] As far as life assurance intermediaries are concerned, the bodies likely to apply for recognition as SROs are the Financial Intermediaries, Managers and Brokers Regulatory Association (FIMBRA) and the Life Assurances and Unit Trust Regulatory Organisation (LAUTRO). Both bodies are currently at work on their rulebooks.

Substantive regulation of life assurance intermediaries

Any lingering hopes nurtured by the life assurance industry that the product and its sales force might escape the reach of proposed investor protection reforms were finally dispelled when Professor Gower published his Discussion Document in 1982.[7] It pointed to the intrinsic investment qualities of life assurance and identified the asymmetries in the regulation of its marketing when viewed alongside the marketing of unit trusts.[8] The problems identified by Professor Gower in his Report relating to the marketing of life assurance arose partly from the diversity of retail outlets, the inability of existing regulation to cover all these outlets and the consequent difficulty of informed investor choice.[9] Life assurance has traditionally been sold by a range of methods, including sales: direct by insurance companies; through tied agents; through a variety of "introducers," such as solicitors and building societies; and through independent intermediaries, some of whom will be brokers registered under the Insurance Brokers (Registration) Act 1977, others of whom will be insurance "advisers" or "consultants."[10] In and of itself, this diversity does not provide a sound reason for regulation. Indeed, numerous buyers and sellers in a particular market are a precondition of its competitive functioning, so, all other considerations being equal, this would be one good reason not to intervene in the retailing of life assurance. However, another precondition to perfect competition is that all market participants should have full and perfect information about the nature and value of the product traded. It is the informational problem in buying life assurance which provides the soundest rationale for regulating its marketing. Again, there is no theoretical reason why the asymmetry of information which exists as between buyers and sellers should constitute a "problem" to trigger regulation. The consumer/investor who finds it difficult or

costly to acquire, or is simply incapable of acquiring, enough information about life assurance products to make his choice should be
able to buy in this service and advice from an independent intermediary—be he "broker," "adviser" or "consultant"—whose
obligation under the law of agency is to proffer advice and products which best meet his clients' requirements anyway. The con-
sumer/investor who feels he has adequate information about the
range of investment products available and the nature of the
investment, and knows what he wants, will go to the company or
one of its agents who offers it, fully aware that that company or
agent is not going to point him to a more suitable product offered
by a competitor.

Two factors are at work in the life assurance market which cause
this model of rational investor behaviour to break down in reality,
so that some kind of regulation is needed. First, it seems that the
very diversity of sellers is causing confusion as to just who is and
who is not a truly independent intermediary, so that investors are
acting on the basis of what they think is independent advice when
in fact it is given by a tied agent or a professional adviser receiving
commission from a particular life office. Secondly, even when the
investor has managed to distinguish between a tied and an independent intermediary the impartiality of the advice offered by the
independent intermediary is, supposedly, affected by the way in
which the intermediary is remunerated. To the extent that commissions payable to the intermediary by the life assurance companies vary as between products, increase with the volume of
business placed by the intermediary with a particular company, or
are indirect in that they take the form of benefits in kind, then the
intermediary has an incentive to advise on the product which will
maximise his total remuneration. If this advice does not coincide
with the best interests of the investor and, even if it does, if he
does not disclose the existence of any additional benefit he gains,
such as increased volume extra commission or a benefit in kind,
then he is in breach of his fiduciary duty as an agent. That is little
comfort for the average investor. He is most probably unaware of
the "common law" rights and duties the principal-agent relation
creates, unaware of their breach (since the benefit to the intermediary is most likely to be undisclosed) and unable or unwilling to
incur the costs of civil action against someone who would probably
prove to be an unattractive defendant in terms of the likelihood of
recovery of damages.

The proposed solution to the first problem, of advisers not being
quite what they seem, is to require all those involved in advising on
or selling life assurance to adopt the mantle either (a) of fully inde-

pendent intermediary, with concomitant responsibilities (basically those of the common law of agency in more comprehensible rule book form), or (b) of company representative, in which case the products of only one company or group can be advised upon and sold. This solution, which has become known as "polarisation" for short, should rectify any confusion investors may have had about the identity and status of retail outlets and so correct information supply which may previously have been sub-optimal, given their particular needs for a decision based on their desired level of information. The fullest description of the justifications for polarisation of life assurance intermediaries can be found in the original proposal from the Securities and Investments Board and the Marketing of Investments Board Organising Committee (SIB-MIBOC) which sees the overall implications as being fourfold, in that it will:

> "— mean that only an independent intermediary will be able to hold himself out as offering a full advisory service on life assurance and unit trusts extending to the products available in the whole market: a company representative will be obliged to make it clear to potential investors that he is restricted to selling the product of the single company or group he represents;
>
> — require the provision of a more rigorous standard of service by many who now hold themselves out as independent intermediaries if they wish to continue to retain that status;
>
> — mean the end of the tied agent as currently understood and commonly encountered in the market; and
>
> — mean that there is no material distinction between company representatives and employees for the purposes of rules relating to the marketing of life assurance and unit trusts."[11]

Employees and representatives of companies offering life assurance products need not of course be individually authorised by the SIB or the relevant SRO to carry on investment business. They will be exempt from the Act's requirement of authorisation by virtue of their status as "appointed representatives" of an authorised principal.[12] The life offices will thus gain authorisation either directly from the SIB or, more likely, from LAUTRO, which must be satisfied that the sales force consisting of appointed representatives will be adequately regulated.[12a] The SIB has published draft rules relating to the conduct of investment business by appointed representatives, and LAUTRO's rulebook will reflect their content.[13] It is clear that the same general standards in the conduct of business as apply to authorised persons also apply to exempt appointed representatives, namely "fair dealing," "know your customer" and "suitability,"[14] along with the requirement to give "best advice." The SIB[15] is aiming at equivalence of regulatory treatment of both "polar" groups—appointed and company representatives and independent intermediaries. Whatever the final content of the LAUTRO rule book turns out to be, one very practical effect will be to ensure much stricter monitoring of appointed representatives, as the authorised life office will be held responsible for any breach of the rules applying to them and satisfactory internal monitoring procedures will be a precondition of membership of LAUTRO. This may lead to a shift in the relationship adopted by life offices and their representatives, with an increase in employment and a decrease in agency, to ensure cheaper monitoring and hence more effective compliance. But the advantages of a self-employed sales force in terms of performance monitoring may be likely still to prevail.

Independent intermediaries will secure authorisation either directly from the SIB or, again more likely, from membership of FIMBRA and will be subject to a much stricter regulatory regime than they are at present. The FIMBRA rulebook is still undergoing revision but the SIB draft rules applying to the conduct of business by authorised firms have been published and, since any SRO must provide at least an equivalent level of regulation as a condition of recognition, a picture can be painted of the types of obligation under which independent life assurance intermediaries will be.

For the purposes of this article, only one question will be asked and answered in any detail of the proposed scheme for independent intermediaries: Does what is proposed effectively correct the information asymmetry between intermediary and investor which is currently distorting investor choice? This question contains within it the further question of the potential conflict of interest arising from the set of incentives operating on an intermediary. If it were not for the fact that the methods of remunerating intermediaries act as a disincentive to comply with the obligations of independent agents, in economic terms the information asymmetry that would then exist would not be significant and would not be an instance of market failure. Indeed, it would be nothing more than the reason an investor would go to an independent intermediary in the first place. It is important to distinguish between, on the one hand, the need for disclosure of enough information about the life assurance product to enable the investor to make an informed decision and, on the other hand, the need to eliminate an intermediary's bias, between different companies' products and different products offered by a company, arising from his remuneration structure. The first need for information does not present a "problem" in the way that the second one does. A rational investor has every incentive to seek out product information of the sort: How does life assurance work? Is it for me? What are the exact financial implications of the many different types of policies on offer? and so on. Given the lack of sophistication of most investors, the almost infinite capacity of the life assurance market for product differentiation and the costs of acquiring such product information, the proposed product disclosure requirements[16] can be seen as a measured regulatory response to this information shortage. A serious confusion has arisen in some of the debate about the regulation of life assurance selling which sees disclosure of the intermediary's commission on products he recommends as an integral part of the more general need for disclosure of product information. An investor is not concerned as to how much the intermediary is making on the side; indeed, to require disclosure of such information might cause more confusion in the mind of the investor and consequent distorted choice, as it is not a product characteristic relevant to investor choice. An investor is, however, very much concerned with the independence of advice he relies on in making his choice and the problem is how to secure that by altering the incentive structures which lead to company and product bias in intermediaries. Disclosure of commission is simply one possible solution. Professor Gower favoured a statutory maximum for commissions payable to intermediaries by life offices and met the "loss to competition" argument by characterising the current commissions competition as not being in the interests of maximising aggregate consumer welfare:

> "Where competition leads to lower commissions it is no doubt generally advantageous to the public to permit insurance companies to compete with one another in the sale of their policies by escalating the commissions which they pay to intermediaries. Such competition must be detrimental to the public as likely to lead to higher prices for policies and, more especially, to less prospect of impartial advice by intermediaries."[17]

The SIB proposals opt for a "voluntary" industry-wide commissions agreement to remove the possibility of bias between subscribing companies in the mind of an intermediary. This agreement will form part of LAUTRO's rulebook and so will be within its realm of responsibility for monitoring and compliance. LAUTRO has now formulated such a commissions agreement and, although subscription to it will not be compulsory for a company, a non-subscribing company must fully disclose the amount of commission payable and must reveal the extent of variance from the agreed commission rates. An investment business which secures direct authorisation from the SIB rather than through membership of LAUTRO, and hence is not a subscriber to the commissions agreement, will also have to make full disclosure of commission payable to the independent intermediary in every case[18]

Commissions disclosure obligations: independent intermediaries

Independent intermediaries are obliged fully to disclose any commission payable to them, whether or not they exceed the maxima stipulated in the LAUTRO commissions agreement and, if so, by how much. However, if the life office paying the intermediary is a subscriber to the LAUTRO maximum commissions agreement, then, from the point of view of the independent intermediary, "it shall be sufficient compliance with this rule if the statement [disclosure] . . . states that fact, and that accordingly the commission payable to the firm in connection with the transaction in question will not exceed those maxima and includes a promise

> "that written particulars of the maximum commissions payable under those rules will be delivered forthwith upon a request for them being made."[19]

In response to the comments of the Director General of Fair Trading the SIB has amended this limited disclosure requirement so that it does not apply at all if the customer has asked the firm what its commission will be. In such a case the intermediary must disclose the full amount of his commission and cannot hide it behind the industry commissions agreement.

To regulate in this way the effect of commissions payable to independent intermediaries is not enough in itself to eliminate company bias, so the SIB has published rules banning non-price competition between the life offices for an independent's business.

The SIB's Draft Rules ban the payment of volume overriders to independent intermediaries. Entering into a reciprocal arrangement to place business with the intermediary and

> "arranging for the making of or the offering to make of gifts to (the independent intermediary) or at his direction the value or frequency of which is such that the gifts can reasonably be expected to influence the judgement of that person in making

recommendations to customers or in making decisions on their behalf . . ."

are also prohibited by the rules.[20]

The star salesman or exclusive agent may still enjoy the company holiday but the independent broker must accept only minimal tokens. To secure further true independence and the elimination of company bias, the SIB will require disclosure of an intermediary's interest in any company the products of which it recommends[21] and vice versa. The FIMBRA rules will at least mirror these requirements as it has a duty, as an SRO, to provide regulatory equivalence with the SIB's Conduct of Business Rules.

The problem of an intermediary's bias between different products of the same company is a more difficult one to control and, unlike company bias, is germane to company agents and employees as well as independent intermediaries. The SIB saw that disclosure of differential commissions in this context would not serve the investors' interests and might be positively harmful, given that the average investor would probably process this information wrongly and opt for the product which paid the lowest commission. Even if investors were not to behave like that, merely requiring disclosure does not actually help them at all. It is irrelevant information in terms of the product information they need in order to come to a decision and does not go to the cause of the problem of product bias. The SIB's general conduct of business rule requires that;

"A firm shall ensure that rates of commission and their frequency of payment and other inducements provided by the firm to its employees, to its appointed representatives and their employees in relation to different products or services marketed by the firm are such that no person who will benefit from these inducements will be likely to be so influenced by them as to recommend to anyone the acquisition of an investment or the effecting of a transaction when to do so would be a breach of any of rules 5.01 to 5.04."[22]

Such a rule will prohibit, for instance, prizes for the best sales figures for a particular product. LAUTRO are more sceptical about the possibility of eliminating product bias, since a leisure preference bias could easily substitute itself for the bias caused by varying commissions and inducements. Some products are simply easier to sell than others and, the argument runs, in the absence of incentives to try otherwise, an intermediary will recommend the product which will guarantee him a sale, and hence commission, rather than a potentially more suitable one which requires more effort from him. To do so would of course be to act in contravention of his general obligation to give "best advice"[23] and ultimately all that any rule concerned with product bias can do is aim to reinforce that obligation by removing direct incentives to breach it. LAUTRO's fears about a new form of product bias ought to be allayed if the obligation to give "best advice" is both meaningfully translated to the industry's sales force and independent intermediaries and vigorously monitored and enforced.

They were wise not even to attempt to set formal, published, "bright line" price standards themselves to control how firms pay and motivate their sales force. That would be a herculean task and would be the type of costly over-regulation one of the main aims of the Financial Services Act must be to avoid. Instead, a combination of industry self-regulation and strict monitoring and enforcement within the context of the conduct of business rules and the general principles underlying them will go as far as it is realistic to expect to be able to go to remove product bias from the retailing of life assurance. Leaving aside the other regulatory changes affecting intermediaries,[24] it is true to say that independent intermediaries will be subject to what may seem like a stricter regulatory regime. However, in fact, the proposed conduct of business rules do not ask of them any higher duty or impose any greater responsibility than they are already subject to under the ordinary law of agency. Mark Weinberg aptly summed up this transition from reliance on the private law of obligations to reliance on regulators:

> "The real change that will come about under the Financial Services Act isn't a change in the law; it's a change in the responsibility for enforcement. Under the legislation, instead of an abstract legal right on the individual, there will be an affirmative system of regulation."[25]

This codification of, and shifting of responsibility for, enforcement of intermediaries' duties should bring about as much, if not more, structural and practical change in the industry as would a change in the content of the common law duty of an agent. The degree of that change should serve as a measure of the extent to which intermediaries' actual business practices have been at variance with the law. One criticism of the specific regulatory reform in issue (and of the whole "Gower to Act" process more generally) which will be discussed at the end of this paper is that no real measurement of the actual extent of market failure and likewise and no real measurement of the costs and benefits of various regulatory responses were undertaken. It is raised here because, had such empirical questions been addressed as part of the review and recommendation process, it would be easier now to predict the likely impact of the new conduct of business rules on intermediaries and investors.

Monitoring, compliance and enforcement

The single most important factor that will determine the efficacy of the proposed regulations is the level of compliance produced by the monitoring and enforcement procedures employed by the SIB and the SROs. If the Act has no practical impact, while one interpretation of this might be that it proves there was nothing amiss in the financial services sector capable of regulatory correction, an equally plausible explanation would be that monitoring and enforcement procedures and policy were such as to create no incentive for individual compliance.

The Act gives the SIB wide powers of investigation into the affairs of an investment business if it has good reason to believe it necessary to exercise them. As an information source from which to draw such reasonable belief, the SIB will rely primarily on returns and spot checks. The SIB has made clear its attitude to monitoring and compliance with its own rules by firms directly authorised by it.[26] It can be expected that the SROs will tailor their monitoring policies to attune with SIBs' approach:

"There will be two principal means of routine monitoring: Inspection visits to firms' places of business and the examination of regular financial returns and other information which firms are required to notify to SIB.

SIB recognises that to many firms (especially the smaller ones) the degree of Financial regulation, monitoring, compliance and audit will be new and that a considerable educational effort will be required to make these arrangements effective. However, it considers the arrangements to be an essential part of the regulatory system and will not hesitate to exercise its powers where it is necessary to do so.

Inspection Visits
All directly regulated firms will be subject to on-site inspection visits, either by SIB's own inspection staff or by persons (eg firms of accountants) whom SIB employs for the task.

Inspection visits will be of two types: regular visits and 'special' visits.

The frequency of regular visits will depend on the nature and extent of a firm's business. However, it is the intention of SIB that firms who have access to client's money or property in the course of their investment business will be visited at least once every two years. Firms which do not handle client's money or property may be visited less frequently. The programme of regular visits will be structured so that regular firms will not know when to expect an inspection in the way they know when to expect their annual external audit. During the course of the inspections, test checks may be carried out to determine the firm's compliance with any aspect of SIB's rules including the Clients' Money Regulations, the Conduct of Business Rules, the Financial Resources Rules, the requirements on unsolicited calls and the Cancellation Rules, although compliance with all the rules will not necessarily be checked in a single visit. In determining the scope and extent of the inspections, due account will be taken of the areas in which auditors provide assurance of firms' compliance and for larger firms, of the extent and nature of firms' own internal compliance reviews. Reports will be prepared from these inspection visits and any necessary follow up action determined and carried out. Such follow-up action may range from a letter of recommended procedural changes to a further investigation or appropriate enforcement or disciplinary action.

'Special' visits will be triggered by a particular concern of the regulater. Such concerns may include among other things, complaints received about a firm, the content of auditors' reports, financial weakness indicated by the financial returns or problems identified in the course of regular visits.

The visits may be short and limited on scope or they may amount to a major investigation. It is intended that a substantial proportion of the inspection staff's time will be reserved for special visits.

Where a firm is a member of an SRO in addition to being authorised by SIB, SIB will co-ordinate its own visits with those of the SRO and will share relevant information which arises."

It does foresee monitoring problems with multiple authorisation of investment businesses, *i.e.* where a firm is directly authorised by the SIB as far as certain types of its business are concerned but obtains authorisation with regard to other types of investment business via membership of one or more SROs. There will be no element of double jeopardy in monitoring as far as members of SROs are concerned, since the SIB does not intend to duplicate the monitoring function of an SRO and "check up" on an SRO's individual monitoring. The different SROs will have monitoring policies which will vary with the nature, size, structure and problems of the membership, but satisfactory monitoring and enforcement procedures are a requirement for recognition as an SRO.[27] There is no regulatory equivalence requirement (as there is with the Conduct of Business Rules and the Powers of Intervention) for an SRO's monitoring and enforcement procedures to match those of the SIB. This is in order to enable an SRO to tailor its monitoring procedures to match its requirements, and SIB have made clear their expectation of effective enforcement from the SROs:

"SIB will also need to be convinced that an SRO has adequate arrangements and resources for the effective monitoring and enforcement of compliance with its rules and with any rules or regulations under Chapter V or Part I of the Act to which members are subject. SIB will be able to come to a view on this "adequacy" only after detailed examination of the arrangements and resources which are or will be at the disposal of an applicant SRO.

SIB will need to be satisfied that an SRO's arrangements for the monitoring of its member firms' conduct and the enforcement of its rules are adequate. It will therefore examine the procedures for inspecting and auditing member firms. It will need to be satisfied that the proposed extent, type and frequency of such inspections and audits (both of financial aspects and of compliance with the rules) are adequate. It will have regard to the arrangements for dealing with breaches of the requirements and rules.

SIB will need to be satisfied that an SRO has effective arrangements for the investigation of complaints from members of the public against its members or itself. It will require details of the procedures which the SRO proposes to adopt with respect to investigating and responding to such complaints."[28]

Will this translate into practice? Again, it is too early to tell, but insofar as life assurance intermediaries are concerned about the type of monitoring to which they will be subject, LAUTRO intends to base its monitoring policy on annual random checks of 33 per cent. of the membership, carrying an enforcement staff of between 12 and 15 people, whereas FIMBRA currently base their monitoring on a combination of close checking of returns and annual random checking of 20 per cent. of their membership.[29]

It may be that these requirements are insufficiently tight to ensure an optimal level of compliance, and the SIB might ask for a revision of FIMBRA's monitoring requirements before recommending its recognition as an SRO under the Financial Services Act. However, it is important for an SRO not to be panicked by the occasional spectacular failure of one of its members into introducing over costly, detailed external monitoring for all of its membership all of the time in an attempt to ensure total and absolute compliance with its rulebook. Such an over inclusive and heavy handed approach would generate costs to the SRO itself, to the membership (who would all devote more resources to compliance and would be more wary of innovation in their investment business) and to investors as a group (as the costs to a regulated firm of transacting business increase, the level of investor demand will fall as investors switch their resources into a less costly activity).[30]

Formal compliance responsibilities will be placed on authorised investment businesses by the SIB to ensure compliance with its conduct of business rules.[31] Firms must initiate and publicise to their staff internal procedures to ensure compliance with the conduct of business rules to which they are subject and keep such procedures under review. An officer or employee of the firm must be given responsibility for conducting regular compliance reviews of the firm's investment business.[32] Such a role will require a blend of detachment from, yet awareness of, the costs of compliance, which may be unrealistic to expect from an individual subject to those same cost constraints himself.

Critique of law reform

Some of the criticisms that will follow are applicable generally throughout the new scheme spawned by the Gower review. "Investor Protection" is an anomalous juxtaposition in one sense, given the unique nature of any financial product: a combination of risk and return. Before regulatory proposals are formulated, it should be the task of anyone charged with that reform to address three questions: (i) what is the purpose of regulating this particular product/market/service? (ii) is regulating a "problem" going to make any difference? and (ii) if so, at what cost?

Gower's stated purpose throughout his Review is "to protect reasonable people from being made fools of,"[33] a lawyer's standard, couched in elastic terms, which should vary from market to market. What does this phrase mean in the context of the marketing of life assurance—is an investor a fool if he fails fully to satisfy himself about the nature of a life assurance contract? If so, who made him a fool? Can any regulation (*e.g.* mandatory disclosure plus cooling-off period) make a significant difference to the fact that that investor does not or will not understand what is on offer and available to him? Will not an over-zealousness in protecting the fool (*e.g.* methods such as restricting cold-calling and advertising) increase costs to "reasonable [rational] people" in the drying up of retail outlets and consequent decreased opportunities and higher cost in investing in life assurance? Is the polarisation of life assurance intermediaries going to put the "reasonable" investor in such a superior position to that in which he was before, when he was able to buy from "the middle ground," that the costs consequent on the reduction in retail outlets will be offset? If so, how? Gower himself admits to one benefit flowing from the diverse and competitive marketing methods which currently exist:

> "The provision of so many outlets for sales of insurance and their introduction into peoples' homes and places of work have helped to ensure that the population of this country is not more under-insured than it is."[34]

It seems that any proposal (be it polarisation, restricted cold-calling or entry control) which even hints at having the effect of reducing competitiveness and increasing costs—whether it be the social cost of under-insurance, an intermediary's or firm's costs in complying with the proposed regulation, the higher cost to the individual investor of the product, or the costs of the regulators themselves[35]—must be the product of a serious attempt to measure the impact in terms of increased costs and benefits of its introduction.

It is this lack of sustained cost/benefit analysis of the need for and effect of new regulation which makes the whole Gower Review process fundamentally flawed and must, to an extent, blight the legislation and rulebook regulation remitting from it.

The Gower review was not informed by any particular economic theory or any independently obtained empirical evidence, only by a basic philosophy in which was exhibited scepticism about the practicability and utility of undertaking any kind of cost/benefit analysis.[36] This is to be regretted, as the recommendations of the report and their implementation in the Financial Services Act are now open to attack from those who see the whole regulatory process *not* as a neutral, perfectly matched correctional response to problems of market failure[37] but, rather, as a response to demand by, and the legitimation of, powerful economic interest groups. "Regulation works to the advantage of the regulated" is the essential thesis of what is loosely described as "capture theory."[38] In its different forms, it ranges from a crude Marxist view of regulation as an oppressive social institution legitimating extant "power" relationships through to a view of regulation as an economic good which producer interest groups can "purchase" from Government in a form which best serves their economic interests. Public regulation of entry into a profession or industry has the same effect on the profits of those already within it as private cartelisation in return for political support.[39] Lacking in edge as these theories may seem to be, they can and do still ground criticisms of specific instances of regulation. These could be met head on if the regulation in question were the product of a two-stage analysis. There should be undertaken, first, an examination of the need for regulation identifying specific market failures and, secondly, an examination of the costs and benefits of different regulatory responses to the problem of market failure. The phenomenon of "regulatory failure" should not be ignored and care should be taken to match the regulatory technique with the problem. For example, the "sledgehammer" of strict licensing requirements may not be the best way to crack the "nut" of inadequate investor information. A major advantage of the structure of the new regulatory scheme is that most of the substantive rule making goes on at SIB and SRO level and there is nothing to prevent these bodies undertaking this type of cost/benefit analysis as an integral part of their rulemaking. The obvious argument against this from a regulator would be the cost of such an exercise, but it ought to be looked upon as an investment in good policy making, and resultant regulation should be able to withstand more scrutiny and criticism than the kind of regulation which emerges from a knee-jerk response to "visible" losses and complaints. The collapses of Norton Warburg and McDonald Wheeler are not *necessarily* proof that regulatory reform is needed. They may be tips of an iceberg or they may simply stand on their own, but it should be part of any regulator's job to find that out and consider the most effective and cheapest response. The kind of cost/benefit or "impact" analysis described here is a precondition to Federal Agency rule making in the United States[40] and has been used by the Australian Law Reform Commission in its report on Insurance Agents and Brokers.[41] Most recently the Government has recommended requiring individual Departments objectively to assess the need for and impact of new regulations on business.[42] This involves three elements:

> "(i) a structural analysis of each new proposal, to be prepared and published by the initiating agency concerned, includ-

ing a systematic assessment of its impact on business enterprise;

(ii) critical scrutiny of the proposal, in particular of the assessment, by a small task force in central Government with real teeth; and

(iii) regular overviews by the task force of proposals in the pipeline and the scope for eliminating, simplifying or rationalising existing requirement systems."[43]

This initiative too is open to criticism on the grounds that it lends too much weight to the measurement of easily assessable compliance costs and does not put sufficient stress on less tangible social costs and benefits of regulation.[44] It is, nonetheless, to be welcomed as the beginnings of "a more objective and systematic approach to the regulatory process."[45] There does not appear to have been any discussion of the need for the SIB and the SROs to comply with this type of regulatory discipline. This is regrettable and it is to be hoped that FIMBRA, LAUTRO and the SIB will perceive that systematic research and analysis, rather than anecdotes, complaints and consultation with interested parties, is always the preferable basis for regulatory action.

Notes

I would like to thank Arthur Selman of the SIB, John Grant of FIMBRA and Malcolm Reid of LAUTRO for giving their time for discussion during the research for this article. However, I remain solely responsible for its contents.

[1] Financial Services Act 1986 (hereafter F.S.A.), Sched. 1, para. 10.

[2] See further Alan Page, "Self-regulation: the Constitutional Dimension" (1986) 49 M.L.R. 141; *Financial Services in the United Kingdom*, Cmnd. 9432 (1985), para. 5.2.

[3] *Review of Investor Protection: Report—Part II* (1985), para. 2.09.

[4] At best this would enhance unoppressive fair decision-making and the proper exercise of discretion within the SIB and the self regulating organisations (SROs), on which see *post*. See in the context of the extension of public law remedies into the area of self-regulation, *R. v. Panel on Take-overs and Mergers, Ex p. Datafin P.L.C.* [1987] 2 W.L.R. 699.

[5] F.S.A., Chap. V.

[6] F.S.A., Sched. 2: Requirements for Recognition of Self-Regulating Organisation.

[7] *Review of Investor Protection: A Discussion Document* (1982).

[8] *Ibid.* paras. 9.01–9.06.

[9] *Review of Investor Protection: Report: Part 1*, Cmnd. 9125 (1984), Chap. 8: "Life Assurance and Unit Trusts."

[10] One of the major criticisms of the Insurance Brokers (Registration) Act 1977 is that it merely regulates the form and not the function of insurance broking, in that it simply prescribes conditions for the use of the title "insurance broker" rather

than regulating the activity, under whatever name it is carried on. See Institute for Fiscal Studies *Insurance: Competition or Regulation* (1986), Chap. 3.

[11] "Life Assurance and Unit Trusts and the Investor", Securities and Investments Board—Marketing of Investments Board Organising Committee (SIB-MIBOC), (April 1986), para. 39.

[12] F.S.A., s.44. S.44(2) defines an appointed representative as a person—

"(a) who is employed by an authorised person (his "principal") under a contract for services which—

(i) requires or permits him to carry on investment business . . . and

(b) for whose activities in carrying on that investment business his principal has accepted responsibility in writing."

S.44(6) makes the principal responsible for the actions of his appointed representatives.

[12a] It is important to note that life offices regulated under the Insurance Companies Act 1982 will still be subject to the prudential supervision of the Department of Trade and Industry as far as their investment management activities are concerned. (FSA s.22). Life offices will only be regulated by the FSA in respect of the marketing and promotion of policies, the management of the investments of pension funds, and the marketing and promotion of contracts for such management and any matters incidental to these two categories of activity. (FSA Sched. 10 para. 4).

[13] "Regulation of Investment Business" (SIB Rule Book) Chapter III Part 6: "Appointed and Company Representatives." Rules 6.02 and 6.03 are designed to ensure polarisation and that appointed and company representatives can be clearly seen only to be selling the products of a company or group.

[14] F.S.A., Sched. 8, and "Life Assurance and Unit Trusts and the Investor" (*supra*, n. 11), para. 21.

[15] The original thinking in this area was done in conjunction with MIBOC (see *supra*, n. 11) under the chairmanship of Mark Weinberg. The two boards have since merged, hence all references to the SIB will often embrace work done by MIBOC too.

[16] Detailed Draft Rules governing product disclosure have yet to be published by the SIB. Their content will require that an investor be given

"(i) information about the nature of the product to enable him to decide whether . . . it has the investment characteristics which he is seeking;

(ii) information to enable him to assess the financial aspects of the investment, *i.e.* the commitment involved; the tax implications; the charges, where identifiable, the surrender values and consequences of early termination; and the ultimate benefits."

(SIB-MIBOC, "Life Assurance and Unit Trusts and the Investor" (April 1986), para. 43).

Some controversy centres around the value of mandatory disclosure of expenses connected with with-profits policies. The view of the SIB and of the Association of British Insurers is that no meaningful investor information about expenses can be formulated, although the SIB is commissioning an independent inquiry to consider disclosure of expenses. (See further SIB-MIBOC, "Product Disclosure; Illustrations, Surrender Values and Past Performance" (July 1986)).

[17] Cmnd. 1925 (1984) (*supra*, n. 9), para. 8.39.

[18] SIB, *Regulation of Investment Business*, Chap. III, Conduct of Business Rules, Draft Rule 5.14.

[19] *Ibid.*, Draft Rule 5.13.

[20] *Ibid.*, Draft Rule 2.05.

[21] *Ibid.*, Draft Rules 2.04 and 5.08.

[22] *Ibid.*, Draft Rule 2.06 (product bias). Rules 5.01 to 5.04 lay down the over-reaching duties to give "Best advice" and provide "Best Execution".

[23] *Ibid.*, Draft Rules 5.01–5.03.

[24] There is not the scope in this article to focus on the various draft SIB rules and regulations governing unsolicited calls, cancellation of life assurance contracts, clients' money accounting practices, advertising and compensation arrangements.

[25] Address to the British Insurance Brokers Association (BIBA) National Conference in Nottingham, April 1986.

[26] SIB, "SIB's Approach to its Regulatory Responsibilities" (February 1987) s. 19, p. 63.

[27] F.S.A., Sched. 2, para. 4.

[28] SIB, "SIB's Approach to its Regulatory Responsibilities" (February 1987) s. 11, pp. 38–39.

[29] Rule 7 of the FIMBRA Rules bases its monitoring policy on requiring audited accounts and checking the financial resources of its members at the point of renewal of membership, as well as random checks of members' records at their place of business.

[30] Criticisms have been voiced recently at FIMBRA's monitoring of its membership in the light of the failure of McDonald Wheeler Fund Management Ltd. This company, a FIMBRA member (and member of the National Association of Securities Dealers and Investment Managers), was put into liquidation in August 1986 and, although the Official Receiver has yet to report finally, the initial report reveals potential heavy investor losses following the mismanagement of funds.

[31] As these compliance requirements form part of the Conduct of Business Rules, there is a duty incumbent on the SROs to maintain equivalence by embodying similar requirements in their rule books.

[32] SIB, "Conduct of Business Rules" (February 1987), Draft Rules 15.01 and 15.02.

[33] Cmnd. 9125 (1984) (*supra*, n. 9), paras. 1.15–1.16.

[34] *Ibid.*, para. 8.18.

[35] All these costs, while individually quantifiable, are obviously interdependent and will reflect each other to an extent.

[36] *Ibid.*, para. 1.16.

[37] The "public interest" theory of regulation. Some classical justifications for regulation are described by Stephen Breyer in "Regulation and its Reform" (Harvard University Press, 1982), pp. 13–36.

[38] For a review of the different versions of capture theory, see R. A. Posner, "Theories of Economic Regulation" (1974) 5 Bell Journal of Economics 335–351.

[39] This theory was first developed by George Stigler in "The Theory of Economic Regulation" (1971) 2 Bell Journal of Economics 3. Some instances of regulation in a European context do seem to bear out his predictions, most notably the Common Agriculture Policy of the EEC. *Quaere*: is it possible to see the Financial Services Act as a market response to this type of political horse-trading? Probably *not*, for the theory would predict a much more restrictive regime of regulation in highly concentrated but heavily branched market sectors (such as the life assurance industry) than will in fact exist.

[40] Federal Register Executive Order 12291 (February 1981), s.2:

"In promulgating new regulations, reviewing existing regulations and developing legislative proposals concerning regulation, all agencies, to the extent permitted by law, shall adhere to the following requirements:
(a) Administrative decisions shall be based on adequate information concerning the need for and consequences of proposed government action;
(b) Regulatory action shall not be undertaken unless the potential benefits to society for the regulation outweigh the potential costs to society;

(c) Regulatory objectives shall be chosen to maximise the net benefits to society;

(d) Among alternative approaches to any given regulatory objective, the alternative involving the least net cost to society shall be chosen; and

(e) Agencies shall set regulatory priorities with the aim of maximising the aggregate net benefits to society, taking into account the condition of the particular industries affected by regulations, the condition of the national economy, and other regulatory actions contemplated for the future."

[41] A.L.R.C. 16 (1980). See also C. G. Veljanovski, "Cost-Benefit and Law Reform in Australia" (1982) 132 N.L.J. 893.

[42] *Burdens on Business: Report of a Scrutiny of Administrative and Legislative Requirements*, (HMSO, March 1985), Chap. 7, and *Lifting the Burden*, Cmnd. 9571 (1986), Chap. 8.

[43] *Ibid.* para. 8.1.

[44] However, see *Burdens on Business* (*supra*, n. 42), Appx. 9, where the contents of impact analysis are described and are to include:

" . . . the costs and benefits of the proposal, quantified where possible. Comprehensive quantification will seldom be feasible, and any estimates will often be subject to major uncertainties. The important point is to identify the key factors on both sides of the equation as an aid to (not a substitute for) the Government's social and political judgment; and to bring out clearly which factors are decisive in determining the line of action proposed . . . "

[45] Cmnd. 9571 (*supra*, n. 42), para. 8.3.

Uberrima Fides in Modern Insurance Law

PAUL MATTHEWS

1. Introduction

Everyone is aware that insurance is one of the contracts in which there is a "duty to be of the utmost good faith."[1] There is, however, surprisingly little more than that which is generally agreed upon, and the duty has been subjected in recent years to considerable criticism.[2] In considering the scope and effect of this duty, a number of different questions arise. It is not possible here to deal exhaustively with the subject,[3] but certain aspects of the duty which have received treatment in recent judicial decisions will be re-examined in the light of those decisions.

2. Source of the Duty

Logically, the first question is: what is the source of the duty? Is it a pre-contractual obligation, a kind of tortious duty operating in the same way as, say, fraudulent misrepresentation,[4] but actually rather more akin to the continental notion of the duty to negotiate in good faith?[5] Is it perhaps the product of a fiduciary relationship between the parties?[6] Is it extra-contractual, but only arising on the formation of the contract? Could it be a collateral contract, or an implied term of the insurance contract itself?[7]

It may, of course, be wondered why this question need be asked at all in 1987. The answer is that the source of a particular legal duty inevitably imbues it with characteristics which have considerable practical impact. For instance, the question of an appropriate limitation period depends on categorisation of the duty as contractual, or tortious, or one of trust, and so on[8] (particularly important is categorisation of a claim as based on "fraud"). Also there are a number of defences to claims based on equitable duties—such as acquiescence, laches, acquisition of third party rights, and so on[9]—which simply do not apply to common law obligations, notwithstanding the fusion of law and equity.[10] The range of potential defendants may be wider or narrower, depending on the cause of action.[11] Remedies, too, may depend on the nature of the right as legal or equitable, proprietary or personal.[12] With this in mind, therefore, let us turn to consider the various possibilities.

It appears that eighteenth-century judges looked on the duty to be of good faith in insurance contracts in the same light as if it were the basis of an action in deceit[13] (which itself had only just been recognised[14]) and early textbook writers adopted this view. Thus:

> "Concealment, or *supressio veri*, is nearly allied to misrepresentation, or *allegatio falsi*, and consists in the suppression of any fact or circumstances material to the risk . . . This, like every other fraud, avoids the contract *ab initio* upon principles of natural justice."[15]

However, this view was repudiated by later nineteenth-century writers. Thus Duer[16] and Arnould[17] took the view that a positive representation on material facts was essential to the contract of insurance—*i.e.* there was an implied term in every contract of insurance that all material facts had been disclosed. In addition Philips[18] held that it was not merely a term, but an implied condition *precedent*. This latter view would explain why an insurance contract was avoided by non-disclosure, whereas the former would not, but would merely produce a breach of contract.[19]

Just as the nineteenth century textbook writers began to draw together all the threads in the cases of different contracts,[20] so the courts began to see "consensus" as the *fons et origo* of every obligation connected with the contract.[21] This naturally led both writers and judges to see such matters as common mistake[22] and frustration[23] (amongst others) in terms of implied conditions precedent: we agree that, if X is the case, then I am/we are to be liable to perform; if not X, then not. Naturally, *uberrima fides* could be seen in the same light, and by the 1880s this was axiomatic. Lord Watson said, in *Blackburn Low* v. *Vigors*[24]:

> "It is in my opinion a condition precedent of every contract of marine insurance that the insured shall make a full disclosure of all facts materially affecting the risk which are within his personal knowledge at the time when the contract is made."[25]

The late nineteenth century was the highwater mark of the consensus view of contractual liability[26] but, even as the judges spoke, the world was changing. The twentieth century, with an interventionist legislature taking more and more pains to spell out the legal consequences (like them or not) of entering this or that transaction,[27] and with the tremendous growth in consumerism,[28] standard form contracts[29] and so on, has seen a considerable retreat from this position.[30] The fiction may be preserved of terms of the

"contract," but the reality is that many "terms" are obligations imposed on the parties.[31] The only consensual act is deciding to enter the transaction at all.[32]

This is not, however, an exclusively modern phenomenon. Part of this process began in the late nineteenth century with the codification of much of English commercial law.[33] In 1906, the law of marine insurance was codified in the Marine Insurance Act 1906, and its provisions included reference to the duty of disclosure of *uberrima fides*.[34] This included reference to a duty "to disclose to the insurer *before the contract is concluded*, every material circumstance which is known to the assured . . . ,"[35] which begins to look like a duty arising outside the contract, although connected with it.

Thus, by 1940 Scott L.J. could say, in *Merchants and Manufacturers Insurance Co.* v. *Hunt*[36]:

> "Even the common law duty of disclosure I find difficult to explain on the theory of its resting only on a implied term of the contract. If it did, it would not arise until the contract had been made; and then its sole operation would be to unmake the contract."

The point did not, it seems, arise for *decision*, however, until 1974, in *March Cabaret* v. *London Assurance*.[37] This was a case where there were argued to be express terms in the policy which were narrower in scope than the ordinary duty of disclosure. May J., citing the dictum of Scott L.J., but not referring to any of the nineteenth-century authorities on the point, held that:

> "Bearing in mind the basis of the rule, however, which is . . . the fact that there is a disparity in negotiating position between the intended assured and insurers, in my judgment the duty to disclose is not based upon an implied term in the contract of insurance at all; it arises outside the contract . . . "[38]

The point arose again in *The Litsion Pride*,[39] in 1985, when Hirst J. considered the conflicting dicta of Scott L.J. in *Merchar and Manufacturers* v. *Hunt*[40] and of Lord Watson in *Blackbu Low* v. *Vigors*.[41] The learned judge held that:

> "The duty not to make fraudulent claims and not to m claims in breach of the duty of utmost good faith is an imp term of the policy, since I prefer the authority of *Blackbu Vigors* in the Court of Appeal (which Lord Watson app in the House of Lords) to the obiter dicta in the *Mer and Manufacturers* case."[42]

However, so far as the doctrine of utmost good faith is con

that case was somewhat unusual, since the facts did not involve a failure to disclose something before the contract was concluded, but rather a failure by the assured to give proper information during the lifetime of the policy relating to war insurance (attracting a higher premium) and also the making of a claim on the insurance (as was held) in circumstances amounting to a fraud on the insurers.

In the most recent decision on this point, *Banque Keyser Ullmann S.A.* v. *Skandia (U.K.) Insurance Ltd.*[43] Steyn J., again without discussing the earlier authorities, held that, in the special circumstances of *The Litsion Pride*,[44] the decision was one concerned with the *scope* of the duty of utmost good faith, rather than with the *source* of the duty. The judge preferred the view of May J. in *March Cabaret*[45] and held that:

> "The body of rules, which are described as the *uberrima fides* principle, are rules of law developed by the judges. The relevant duties apply before the contract comes into existence, and they apply to every contract of insurance. In my judgment it is incorrect to categorise them as implied terms, in the sense in which the [assureds] seek to do so. I also reject the contention that these rules only become applicable by way of a collateral contract."[46]

It is unfortunate that the learned judge did not discuss the earlier authorities, which were cited to him and which, it is submitted, were binding on him.

If, however, as the most recent case holds, the source of the duty of utmost good faith is to be found outside the contract, and indeed before it comes into existence, and is not a collateral contract, what then is its juridical basis?

One candidate might be thought to be a fiduciary relationship between the parties. This originally arose where one person entrusted either his property or some important task on his behalf to another.[47] In modern times the concept of the fiduciary relationship has been much extended in English law—for example, to the case of unauthorised and self-appointed agents[48]—and it has been judicially stated that the categories of fiduciary relationships are not closed.[49] Modern opinion is that a fiduciary relationship occurs (in a broad sense) when one person is entrusted with some power by another, which power will in some material way affect that other once it is exercised.[50]

American insurance case law has, as might be expected, already had to deal with this question. The American courts (and particularly the more adventurous jurisdictions among them) readily

accepted that a liability insurer stood in a fiduciary relationship with the insured, at least in cases where the insurer had power to take over the insured's legal defence and to settle claims made against him.[51] One aspect of that fiduciary relationship was the insurer's own duty to disclose relevant matters to the insured. Thus, in one case, the Court of Appeals of California said:

> "An insurer has a special relationship with its insureds and, among other things, owes to its insureds, the implied-in-law duty just mentioned . . . This duty is fiduciary in nature . . . and any breach of it to the advantage of the person in fault that misleads another to its prejudice amounts to constructive fraud . . . A form of such fraud is the non-disclosure by the fiduciary of relevant matters arising from the relationship . . . "[52]

One important feature to notice from this quotation is that in that case it was the *insurer* who was said to owe fiduciary duties to the *insured*. This is important in the light of the discussion hereafter[53] as to whether the duty to be of the utmost good faith is indeed reciprocal and applies just as much to insurers as to insureds.

Whilst it is easy to see why a liability insurer should be held to stand in a fiduciary position *vis-à-vis* his insured, especially in relation to conduct of the insured's defence, it might be thought more difficult to take the same view of the duties owed by an insurer in other kinds of insurance (*e.g.* fire or disability insurance). However, the distinction between the different types of insurer has been whittled away to immateriality. American courts have held that insurers, by reason of their special position, owe similar duties to all insureds,[54] and accordingly the insurer/insured relationship has been categorised as fiduciary, even in non-liability insurance.[55]

Up until recently, it does not appear to have been argued in an English court that the relationship between insurer and insured was in any way fiduciary. However in *Banque Keyser Ullmann* v. *Skandia*,[56] the point was argued at some length, and the American authorities were cited. As Steyn J. found for the insureds against the insurers on other grounds, he did not consider in great detail the merits of the argument that insurers were in a fiduciary position to the insureds, but merely concluded that no cause of action based on breach of fiduciary duty was sustainable on the facts of that case.[57]

That case involved policies of guarantee insurance granted by insurers to secure banks in the event of non-repayment of loans being made to certain borrowers. It was alleged on behalf of the banks (and, as the judge held, proved) that the underwriter employed by the lead insurer knew before entering certain of the transactions that the broker retained by the banks had acted fraudulently in relation to similar insurance shortly before, had deceived his own clients as to the extent of the cover, and yet failed to alert the banks as to these facts. The loans went into default, the insurers refused to pay on the grounds of fraud, and the banks claimed to be compensated for the failure of the lead insurer to inform them of what its employee knew.

These facts were strong and, save for the fact that the insurers were not liability insurers, with the power to sue or defend legal proceedings in the name of the insured, it is difficult to think of circumstances more amenable to a successful claim for the existence of a fiduciary relationship between insurer and insured. However, as mentioned above, Steyn J. merely recorded that no cause of action was sustainable on the facts.

It is nonetheless submitted that a liability insurer, at least, exhibits some of the characteristics of a fiduciary, in that he has power to bind the insured, for example by taking a decision as to when and at what level to settle claims made against him. The position with other insurers is less clear. It may be that, where a potential lender is looking to an insurer for guarantee insurance, and the insurer knows that the lender will not lend without such insurance, the insurer could be said to be in a position of power *vis-à-vis* the lender: effectively, he has the power either to prevent the loan or to allow it to go ahead. Furthermore, in such circumstances, the insurer is vitally interested in allowing the loan to go ahead, for then he will obtain the insurance premium. In failing to pass on information which it is material for the insured to know, the insurer is allowing his duty to the insured (it may be argued) to conflict with his interest in receiving the premium, a classic characteristic of breaches of fiduciary duty.[58]

There may, therefore, be thought something to be said for seeing the basis of the duty to be of good faith, in modern times, as a fiduciary relationship, at least so far as the insurer is concerned. There is, however, the insured to be considered. Even if the insurer is a fiduciary for the insured, so as to explain his duty of good faith, are there similar fiduciary obligations attaching to the *insured*, so as to justify *his* duty of good faith? This at first sight seems more difficult to argue. In the conventional insurance transaction, the insured has very little power to bind the insurer by what he does, as it is commonly expressly provided that, if the insured does anything to confirm or increase the insured loss (*e.g.* by admission of liability to a third party, or by failing to take steps to minimise damage), then the insurance may be avoided by the insurer. However, it may be that the nature of insurance itself demands such obligations of the insured, and the words merely make express what would anyway be implied. The insured is, after all, commonly in control of the situation in a way which the insurer is not. If that is so, the fact of the insured's already owing duties to the insurer to minimise the insurer's risk is a substantial pointer to the insured being a kind of fiduciary for the insurer,[59] a further characteristic of that relationship being the duty to disclose to the insurer at the outset all facts material to the risk.

There is nothing wrong in principle with two parties in a contractual relationship being fiduciaries for each other: partnership is the obvious example.[60] On the other hand, that is not to say that all business arrangements must create fiduciary relationships, and indeed the High Court of Australia recently refused to find such a relationship between a manufacturer and a distributor.[61] But a transaction such as insurance is rather special: each side has a certain measure of advantage over the other, whether knowledge or some other form of power, and the law of insurance does seek so far as possible to prevent that advantage being taken.

Of course, it is possible that the duty to be of the utmost good faith could be grounded, not in a fiduciary relationship as such, but on some other principles of equity. There are, for example, independent equitable principles which bear some resemblance to the duty to be of utmost good faith, at least in its "disclosure" manifestation, in the difficult area of law sometimes known as "proprietary" estoppel. (In truth, the estoppel extends much wider than cases of property, but goes at least as far as cases of simple obligation. The important fact to note is that it cannot be estoppel *at common law*, because it involves having a *duty to speak*, which common law estoppel would not countenance.[62]) Thus:

> "If a stranger begins to build on my land supposing it to be his own, and I, perceiving his mistake, abstain from setting him right, and leave him to persevere in his error, a Court of Equity will not allow me afterwards to assert my title to the land on which he had expended money on the supposition that the land was his own. It considers that, when I saw the mistake into which he had fallen, it was my duty to be active and to state my adverse title; and that it would be dishonest in me to remain wilfully passive on such an occasion, in order afterwards to profit by the mistake which I might have prevented."[63]

To take the matter out of the realms of property:

> "If A sees B acting in the mistaken belief that A is under some

binding obligation to him and in a manner consistent only with the existence of such an obligation, which would be to B's disadvantage if A were thereafter to deny the obligation, A is under a duty to B to disclose the non-existence of the supposed obligation."[64]

Indeed, some textbook writers go further than this, and refer simply to a mistake of one negotiating party perceived by the other as to some matter vital to the contract in question, when the perceiving part may come under an obligation to correct the mistake.[65]

All of these examples are very interesting but fundamentally, and notwithstanding that they arise in equity rather than at law, they depend on an analogy with fraud, because it is necessary that one party *know* that the other party is mistaken. From this, one can well understand how it was possible in the eighteenth century to draw the analogy with fraud (which at common law would depend on positive statements which were untrue), and hold there to be a duty to speak when one party was aware that the other party was acting or was about to act upon a false premiss.[66]

But this will not do for our case, because the duty to be of the utmost good faith does not depend nowadays on actual knowledge by one party to the transaction of some material fact. He may have known it once, and now have forgotten it.[67] Or he may never have known it at all, although it would have been easy for him to discover it,[68] or perhaps he ought to have known of it and may be said "constructively" to have known it.[69] In all these cases the equitable principles above discussed would not apply, because there would be no actual knowledge.[70] Yet it seems that a party in such cases would still be under a duty to disclose material facts for the purposes of the *uberrima fides* principle,[71] and if he failed to do so the same legal consequences would flow.

If the source of the duty is not equity, then the search must turn to another direction. Clearly, circumstances may be such that one party to the insurance relationship may owe a duty of care to the other such that, should he fail to warn the other of some fact which is within his knowledge but outside the knowledge of the other, he will be liable in negligence.[72] Indeed, this was one of the grounds upon which Steyn J. held in favour of the insured banks in *Banque Keyser Ullmann* v. *Skandia*.[73] However, it does not by itself explain the existence of utmost good faith duties which, as the learned judge in that case held, are conceptually distinct, and indeed formed an entirely separate ground of recovery for the banks against the insurers.

The problem is that, once one: (*a*) rejects the insurance contract itself as a source of obligation; (*b*) abandons any idea of the duties being based on fraud, and (*c*) declines to see the duty as the child of equity, it is very difficult to know where further to look. Steyn J. in *Banque Keyser Ullmann* v. *Skandia* seemed to be thinking of an independent source of legal obligation. It is tempting to look at it in terms of the "law merchant," imported into English law in the seventeenth and eighteenth centuries.[74] But, although this is tempting, because of the importance of the role of *uberrima fides* in insurance and suretyship transactions, it is beyond question that the principles had, and continue to have, a role to play in relation to other areas of the law, such as family arrangements[75] and company prospectuses,[76] which did not develop out of the law merchant but, rather, from the courts of equity.

In the end, the difficulty which we face is this. We live in an age of rapidly developing legal theory and legal techniques, and in which commentators have announced (and in some cases judges have espoused) the "death of contract,"[77] the fusion of contract and tort,[78] and the emergence of a "law of restitution,"[79] amongst other events. Yet we depend for our judicial decision making upon authorities stretching back 200 years or more, reflecting different aspirations and objectives as society has changed.

Judged by the standards of the nineteenth century, the answer to our question would have been obvious; all such obligations as those with which we are now concerned would have been regarded as arising from the fact of contract.[80] In modern times, however, commentators see obligations arising in any way but through the fact of contract. Steyn J.'s attempts, in *Banque Keyser Ullmann* v. *Skandia*, to locate the source of the duty to be of the utmost good faith somewhere other than in contract is simply a reflection of this modern attitude. Unfortunately, so long as we have different rules for dealing with substantive rules from different sources this difficult and sometimes fruitless exercise must be gone through. As a matter of *authority*, it is submitted that May J. and Steyn J. were wrong, and Hirst J. right: the only clearly legally justifiable source of the utmost good faith duty at the present day still remains the contract itself.

3. *Reciprocity*

The next question is the extent to which the duty to be of good faith can be said to apply to insurer as it does to insured. That the duty to be of good faith applies mainly to conduct of the insured cannot be doubted, but there is a surprising dearth of case-law dealing with an insurer's duty to be of good faith towards his insured.

Notwithstanding this lack of authority, the textbooks[81] say that, in principle, the insurer owes a like duty to be of the utmost good faith as the insured owes to the insurer. The reason is that the justification for the duty to apply to the insured applies just as much to the insurer himself. Usually, as Lord Mansfield pointed out in the leading case of *Carter* v. *Boehm*[82]:

> "The special facts, upon which the contingent chance is to be computed, lie . . . in the knowledge of the insured only: the underwriter trusts to his representation, and proceeds upon the confidence that he does not keep back any circumstance in his knowledge, to mislead the underwriter into a belief that the circumstance does not exist, and to induce him to estimate the *risque* as if it did not exist."

But it is quite possible, at least in principle, for there to be a case where the special facts are within the knowledge of the *insurer*, and outside that of the insured. Thus, Lord Mansfield, again, said:

> "The policy would equally be void, against the underwriter, if he concealed; as, if he insured a ship on her voyage, which he privately knew to be arrived: and an action would lie to recover the premium."[83]

Yet although there are a number of judicial dicta to the effect that the duty applies to insurer as to insured,[84] there appeared until very recently to be no reported case in any common law jurisdiction (including the United States of America) in which an insurer was held to have breached his duty to be of good faith towards his insured.

In *Banque Keyser Ullmann* v. *Skandia*,[85] as has been mentioned, the leading underwriter discovered that the proposed insured's broker had, in relation to identical transactions a few months earlier, deliberately deceived his clients as to the very existence of cover, on the faith of which they had acted to their considerable prejudice. Here was something which the insurer knew, and the insured did not, as they prepared to enter into further transactions of the same kind, broked by the same fraudulent broker. The insurance in these further transactions turned out to be fraudulently obtained, in similar (though not identical) ways. The insured banks, on discovering these facts, not unnaturally complained that the insurers, knowing facts most material to the risk, ought to have told them what they knew, and in not doing so had breached their duty to be of the utmost good faith.

We shall return to this case later, but what is presently note-worthy is that the insurers attempted to deny that the duty to be of good faith applied to insurers at all, and only applied to the insured. To do so, they first had to get over the fact that, in codifying the law of marine insurance in the Act of 1906, Parliament had enacted the rule of *uberrima fides* in terms applying to both parties:

> "If the utmost good faith be not observed by either party, the contract may be avoided by the other party."[86]

As to this, Steyn J. said:

> "The Act was a codification of the common law, and it is inconceivable that the common law regarded marine insurers as bound by a duty of the utmost good faith but not other insurers."[87]

The learned judge concluded:

> "It is difficult to imagine a more retrograde step, subversive of the standing of our insurance law and our insurance markets, than a ruling today that the great judge erred in *Carter* v. *Boehm* in stating the principle of good faith rests on both parties. I unhesitatingly reject this contention."[88]

It is submitted that Steyn J. was right to do so. Insurance is, as Lord Mansfield recognised in *Carter* v. *Boehm*,[89] a transaction of a speculative nature. Each party assesses its position on the basis of all the available information. The insurer will accept the risk only if he can assess its likelihood of maturing, so as to be able to calculate an acceptable premium. The insured will lay off the risk only if, having assessed the likelihood of its maturing, he needs to dispose of the risk more than he needs to retain the premium. It is not more of a speculation on the one side than the other, but exactly the same speculation seen from two sides. Each party needs the same information, and it would therefore be nonsense for the law to require one party to supply all its relevant information to the other, but to cast no duty on that other to reciprocate.

4. *Content*

The duty to be of good faith usually demonstrates itself in relation to disclosure by one party to another of information in the hands of the first of which the second is ignorant. That is not to say that there cannot be other manifestations, such as a duty on insurers to set out proposal forms fairly and in a way which does not mis-lead,[90] or on the insured not to make claims in bad faith,[91] but such cases are of less significance.

From the point of view of the potential insured, the duty to be of the utmost good faith means that he must disclose to the insurer all facts material to the risk within his knowledge, being facts which the insurer neither knows nor is by law treated as knowing.[92] He is not, however, bound to disclose facts which arise or come to his knowledge after the insurance contract has been made,[93] unless a policy is renewed, which in law amounts to a new contract.[94] Neither is he bound to disclose facts which reduce the risk,[95] or disclosure of which is waived by the insurer.[96]

The test of *materiality* has been the subject of a certain amount of judicial disagreement. In particular, there was until recently a debate as to whether the facts not disclosed must have caused the particular insurer to alter his decision to insure on the terms actually transacted,[97] or whether it was sufficient to say that the facts, if disclosed, would have been *taken into account* (not necess-arily to change his mind) by the underwriter, and not the particular underwriter at that, but by a notional and hypothetical under-writer.[98] Recent authority has, however, made it clear that it is the latter view which is to prevail, both in marine[99] and non-marine[1] cases.

In relation to the duty of an *insurer* to disclose material facts to an insured, a similar test can be formulated. In *Banque Keyser Ull-mann* v. *Skandia*,[2] Steyn J. said:

> "In considering the ambit of the duty of disclosure of the insurers, the starting point seems to me as follows: in a proper case it will cover matters peculiarly within the knowledge of the insurers, which the insurers know that the insured is ignor-ant of and unable to discover, but which are material in the sense of being calculated to influence the decision of the insured to conclude the contract of insurance. In considering whether the duty of disclosure is activated in a given case a Court ought in my judgment to test any provisional conclu-sion by asking the simple question: Did good faith and fair dealing require a disclosure?"

Of course, this does not mean that an insurer must tell an insured absolutely everything which it knows about a proposed risk. But there will clearly be cases where the insurer knows very much more than the insured of the facts on which an assessment of the risk is to be carried out, if only because the insurer deals with the subject-matter every day and the insured but rarely. Alternatively, and as in *Banque Keyser Ullmann* v. *Skandia* itself, it may be that the insurer has information relating to the probity of a person involved in the transaction, which may impinge on the validity or the extent of the cover itself. Thus, as the learned judge said in that case:

> "If good faith and fair dealing has any meaning at all it seems to me that there was a clear duty on [the underwriters] to place the relevant facts before the banks" [*i.e.* the insured].[3]

5. *Remedies*

The traditional view has always been that the remedy for a breach of the duty of utmost good faith by way of non-disclosure lies in avoidance of the insurance policy.[4] This avoidance takes place *ab initio*, so that the contract is treated as though it never existed.[5] On the other hand, unless and until the right to avoid is exercised, the courts will treat the insurance contract as subsisting.[6] This is a similar remedy to that which existed at common law for fraudulent misrepresentation[7] and in equity even for innocent[8] misrepresentation. Coupled with avoidance in insurance cases (and like the equitable remedy of rescission), there could be recovery of any premium or other monies paid on the footing of a valid insurance,[9] except that an insured could not recover his premium where there had been fraudulent non-disclosure.[10] Lord Mansfield was clear in *Carter* v. *Boehm*[11] that, if avoidance of the insurance came about by reason of the *insurer's* non-disclosure, there would be recovery of premium by the insured. However, whereas in the equitable remedy of rescission the basis of return of monies paid was simple equitable restitution,[12] in insurance cases the basis of return of monies paid was quasi-contractual, *i.e.* monies paid on a failure of consideration.[13]

Notwithstanding the emphasis laid by the authorities on avoidance as a remedy, it is clear that other remedies are, in principle at least, possible. Thus, in *Kettlewell* v. *Refuge Assurance*[14] Lord Alverstone C.J. allowed an insured to recover her premiums on two grounds, one being fraudulent misrepresentation on behalf of the insurer, and in *London Assurance* v. *Clare*[15] it was suggested (*obiter*) that an insurer might sue the insured for damages where a fraudulent claim was put forward. Since 1963,[16] the same could be said of negligent misrepresentation and, since 1967,[17] of certain innocent misrepresentations. If there is for some reason a duty to speak, such an (actionable) misrepresentation may happen through silence,[18] or an estoppel may be founded.[19]

It might also be thought at least arguable that the duty to disclose information material to the risk might be enforceable in a different way—that is, by injunction—by analogy with the so called "ship's papers" cases, where orders are made for delivery up of the ship's documents at an early stage in proceedings to enforce a claim under a policy of marine insurance.[20] These orders are in effect a means of ensuring that underwriters were fully informed of all material facts, as they were entitled under the duty to be of the utmost good faith.[21] If an injunction might be granted, there must have been jurisdiction to award damages in lieu of an injunction, under the successor provisions to Lord Cairns' Act.[22] In *Banque Keyser Ullmann* v. *Skandia*,[23] this point was in fact argued, but, without giving detailed reasons, Steyn J. held merely that such an argument was unsustainable on the facts of that case.[24]

Leaving aside the "ship's papers" and injunction route, which may be thought somewhat tortuous, and returning to the direct point, there would seem to be no reason in principle why, in an appropriate case, *damages* might not be awarded for breach of the duty to be of the utmost good faith. Damages is after all the primary common law remedy,[25] and the duty of *uberrima fides* is one well known to common law courts. However, two principal points may be urged against this view.

The first relates to the Marine Insurance Act 1906, which, although it deals specifically with the law relating to marine insurance, has been said judicially to have codified many of the principles of general insurance law.[26] It may be argued that nowhere in the 1906 Act is any mention made of damages as a remedy for breach of the duty to be of utmost good faith. The only remedies mentioned are avoidance and return of premium.[27] But Chalmers, in drafting the Act, as with other Acts prepared originally by him,[28] did not purport to state the whole law relating to contracts of marine insurance.[29] For instance, he did not say that, if an insured breached an express warranty of non-disclosure, the insurer might have an action for breach of contract, though obviously he might. Nor did he say that either party might sue for damages for fraud.[30] Indeed, the learned draughtsman expressly said that the Act was *not* to be treated as a complete code.[31] Furthermore, it is difficult to see how there could be many cases where avoidance and return of premium would not do justice, and thus the problem would not have been present to anyone's mind. In any event it must be borne in mind that a Victorian draughtsman, however eminent, might occasionally see things in too restrictive a light, or even might simply err.[32]

The second point to be considered is a dictum of Scrutton J. in

Glasgow Assurance Corporation v. *William Symondson & Co.*[33] In that case, underwriters claimed against insurance brokers to be entitled to set aside a treaty and all policies effected under it, by reason of the non-disclosure of the broker's intention to declare his own underwriting partners as assureds (who would then make a profit by difference of premiums). That claim failed. But Scrutton J. added:

> "If I had found concealment of a material fact, the plaintiffs would have had to face the question, to which in my opinion they gave no satisfactory answer, as to how they could cancel the policies when underwriters, parties to them . . . were not before the court; for non-disclosure is not a breach of a contract giving rise to a claim for damages, but a ground of avoiding a contract."[34]

In *Banque Keyser Ullmann* v. *Skandia*,[35] where a claim was made for *damages* for breach of the duty of utmost good faith, Steyn J. considered how much weight this dictum should carry in reaching his own decision. The learned judge held[36] that there were four factors lessening the importance of that dictum: first, there was no material non-disclosure, and the point did not arise; secondly, there was no claim for damages; thirdly, there was no argument that damages were recoverable for breach of utmost good faith; fourthly, Scrutton J. said that non-disclosure was not *a breach of contract* giving rise to damages, rather than simply not actionable in damages. Steyn J. also added that in any event not all the necessary parties were before the court.

It would appear that *Banque Keyser Ullmann* v. *Skandia* is the first where it has been considered, with full argument, whether damages should in principle be available for breach of the duty of utmost good faith. The learned judge considered the matter from the point of view of legal principle and of policy. The judge said:

> "Once it is accepted that the principle of the utmost good faith imposes meaningful reciprocal duties, owed by the insured to the insurers and vice versa, it seems anomalous that there should be no claim for damages for breach of those duties in a case where that is the only effective remedy. The principle *ubi jus ibi remedium* succinctly expresses the policy of our law."[37]

The judge was, however, concerned by the rule regarding materiality of non-disclosure: it is not the actual effect of non-disclosure on the particular underwriter, but the effect on the prudent (and notional) underwriter. Steyn J. asked himself how, if the test of materiality from the insured's point of view was the effect on the notional insured only, *damages* could be awarded if the non-disclosure had no effect on the actual insured. He concluded:

> "In my judgment the only conceivable answer is that the requirements for avoidance are less than for an action for damages . . . In order to claim damages on the ground of a breach of the obligation of the utmost good faith it will in my judgment be incumbent on the insured to prove that the non-disclosure induced him to enter into the contract."[38]

Obviously, damages for breach of the duty to be of the utmost good faith cannot be claimed unless that breach has caused a loss; it is difficult to see how that could be so unless the non-disclosure (the breach) caused the insured to enter the contract, but it is respectfully submitted that it is the principles of causation which should properly govern this part of the law and not the principles of reliance.[39]

The learned judge concluded:

> "Plainly, the problem confronting me is a novel one. Occasionally, judges have to apply an existing remedy to a new situation when a right already recognised by the law is not adequately protected. . . . In my judgment justice and policy considerations combine in requiring me to rule that in principle an insured can claim damages from an insurer arising from loss suffered by the insured as a result of a breach of the obligation of the utmost good faith by the insurer."[40]

It is submitted that this is a sensible and just result.

6. *Conclusion*

The principle of *uberrima fides* is a curious animal: arising from an indefinite source, with an undetermined content, and applying to a small (but nonetheless uncertain) range of situations, it has in consequence considerable flexibility and versatility. It can be—and is—prayed in aid in circumstances where a higher standard than usual of commercial morality is needed to enable parties to deal fairly with each other. In the recent cases discussed above, this principle has been shown to be full if vitality and, indeed, has been developed and extended, notably in relation to the question of remedies. Notwithstanding Parliament's ceaseless amendment of the law by statutory means, this reassertion of the scope and power of judicial law-making is very welcome: long may it continue.

Notes

[1] Others include suretyship, family arrangements, and contracts to take shares in new companies: see, *e.g. March Cabaret* v. *London Assurance* [1975] 1 Lloyd's Rep. 169 at 175 col. 2, and Chitty, *Contracts*, (25th ed., 1983), ("Chitty") vol. 1, para. 460.

[2] See, *e.g.* Law Reform Committee, 5th Report, Cmnd. 62 (1957); Hasson, (1969) 32 M.L.R. 615; *Lambert* v. *Co-Operative Insurance Services* [1975] 2 Lloyd's Rep. 465; Law Commission Report No. 104 (1980). Some of these criticisms may be dealt with if a long proposed EEC Directive on aspects of insurance is ever promulgated. In an apparently successful attempt to ward off legislative intervention, the insurance industry has recently produced *Revised Statements of Insurance Practice*, but these are narrow in scope and have no legal force: see Forte (1986) 49 M.L.R. 754, and Birds, "Self-regulation and Insurance Contracts", *ante*, Chap. 1.

[3] See, *inter alia*, MacGillivray and Parkington *Insurance Law* (9th ed., 1981) ("MacGillivray and Parkington"), paras. 524, 614–705; Birds, *Modern Insurance Law*, (1982) ("Birds") pp. 83–104; Halsbury's *Laws of England* (4th ed., 1978), vol. 25 ("Halsbury"), paras. 365–378; Chitty, vol. 2, paras. 3684–3692; Colinvaux, *The Law of Insurance* (5th ed., 1984) ("Colinvaux"), Chap. 5.

[4] *Cf. De Costa* v. *Scandret* (1723) 2 P.Wms. 169; *Seamen* v. *Fonereau* (1749) 2 Str. 183; *Pawson* v. *Watson* (1778) 2 Cowp. 785; *Bize* v. *Fletcher* (1779) 1 Dougl. 12n.

[5] See, *e.g.* Nicholas, *French Law of Contract* (1982), at pp. 67–69; and *cf. Comfort* v. *Fowke* (1840) 6 M. & W. 358 at p. 379. The judgment of Farwell L.J. in *Re Bradley and Essex and Suffolk Accident Indemnity Society* [1912] 1 K.B. 415 at p. 430 comes close to this.

[6] See *post*, pp. 42–45.

[7] See *post*, pp. 40–42.

[8] See, *e.g. Chesworth* v. *Farrar* [1967] 1 Q.B. 407.

[9] See Snell's *Equity* (28th ed., 1982), at pp. 36–37 (acquiescence), 34–37 (laches), 48–58 (third parties).

[10] *Cf. United Scientific Holdings* v. *Burnley Borough Council* [1978] A.C. 904 at p. 924, and the Preface to the second edition of Meagher, Gummow and Lehane, *Equity—Doctrines and Remedies* (1984), ("Meagher Gummow and Lehane").

[11] *E.g.* the wrongdoing of an agent may affect his principals if characterised as contractual, but not if tortious: *cf. Banque Keyser Ullmann S.A.* v. *Skandia (UK) Ltd.*, *infra*, n. 46.

[12] See, *e.g.* Khurshid & Matthews, (1979) 95 L.Q.R. 79.

[13] See the authorities cited *supra* in note 4.

[14] *Pasley* v. *Freeman* (1789) 3 T.R. 51.

[15] Marshall, *Insurance* (2nd ed., 1808), at p. 464; see also Park, *Marine Insurance* (4th ed., 1800), at p. 174.

[16] 2 *Insurance*, at pp. 648–655.

[17] *Marine Insurance* (2nd ed.), vol. 1, at p. 549.

[18] 1 Phillips, *Insurance*, s.537.

[19] *Blackburn Low* v. *Vigors* (1887) 12 App.Cas. 531.

[20] See, *e.g.* Chitty (1st ed., 1826).

[21] See, *e.g. Rumsey* v. *N.E. Railway Co.* (1863) 14 C.B. (N.S.) 596; *Haynes* v. *Haynes* (1869) 1 Dr. & Sm. 426 at p. 433; *The Moorcock* (1889) 14 P.D. 64.

[22] *Couturier* v. *Hastie* (1856) 5 H.L.C. 673.

[23] *Taylor* v. *Caldwell* (1863) 3 B. & S. 826.

[24] (1887) 12 App.Cas. 531.

[25] *Ibid.* at p. 539.

[26] See, *e.g.* Anson, *Law of Contract* (1st ed., 1879): Pollock, *Principles of Contract* (1st ed., 1876).

[27] See, *e.g.* Increase of Rent and Mortgage Interest (Restrictions) Act 1920; Moneylenders Acts 1900–1927.

[28] Reflected in recent years by the Misrepresentation Act 1967, the Fair Trading Act 1973, the Consumer Credit Act 1974, the Restrictive Trade Practices Acts 1976 and 1977, the Unfair Contract Terms Act 1977, and the Competition Act 1980.

[29] *Cf. L'Estrange* v. *Graucob* [1934] 2 K.B. 394.

[30] *Cf.* Lord Radcliffe's speech in *Davis Contractors* v. *Fareham U.D.C.* [1956] A.C. 696.

[31] See Goode, *Commercial Law* (1982) ("Goode"), at pp. 41–42.

[32] One might as well say that motor car drivers by taking their cars out on the roads impliedly undertake to compensate the victims of their negligence: such a "contract" would be hardly less consensual.

[33] *E.g.* in the Bills of Exchange Act 1882, the Partnership Act 1890, and the Sale of Goods Act 1893.

[34] Ss.17, 18 (the Act is cited hereafter as "M.I.A.").

[35] S.18(1) (Emphasis added).

[36] [1941] K.B. 295 at p. 313.

[37] [1975] 1 Lloyd's Rep. 437.

[38] *Ibid.* at p. 518 col. 2 to p. 519 col. 1.

[39] [1985] 1 Lloyd's Rep. 437.

[40] *Supra*, n. 36.

[41] *Supra*, n. 25.

[42] [1985] 1 Lloyd's Rep. 437 at p. 518 col. 2 to p. 519 col. 1.

[43] [1987] 1 Lloyd's Rep. 69; [1987] 1 L.M.C.L.Q. 5.

[44] *Supra*, n. 39.

[45] *Supra*, n. 37.

[46] [1987] 1 Lloyd's Rep. 69, 94.

[47] See *per* Asquith L.J. in *Reading* v. *A.G.* [1949] 2 All E.R. 68 at p. 70.

[48] *English* v. *Dedham Vale Properties Ltd.* [1978] 1 W.L.R. 93.

[49] *Ibid.* at p. 110F.

[50] See, *e.g.* Shepherd (1981) 97 L.Q.R. 51 at pp. 68–71, 75.

[51] See *Crisci* v. *Security Insurance Co.* 426 P.2d. 173 (1967) (Calif. S.C.); *Gruenberg* v. *Aetna Insurance Co.* 510 P.2d. 1032 (1973) (Calif.S.C.), *per* Roth J. (dissenting); *Florida Farm Bureau* v. *Rice* 393 So.2d. 552 (1980) (Florida C.A.).

[52] *Spindle* v. *Chubb/Pacific Indemnity Group* (1979) 152 Cal.Rptr. 776, 780.

[53] *Post*, pp. 44–45.

[54] *Gruenberg* v. *Aetna Insurance Co.*, *supra*, n. 51, *per curiam*; *Egan* v. *Mutual of Omaha Insurance Co.*, 598 P.2d. 452 (1979) (Calif.S.C.); *Hoskins* v. *Aetna Life Insurance Co.*, 452 N.E.2d. 1315 (1983) (Ohio S.C.).

[55] *Egan* v. *Mutual of Omaha Insurance Co.*, *supra*, n. 54 (disability policy).

[56] *Supra*, n. 43.

[57] *Ibid.* at p. 102.

[58] See Meagher, Gummow and Lehane, at para. 504; Goff and Jones, *The Law of Restitution* (3rd ed., 1986) ("Goff and Jones"), at pp. 632–635; Shepherd, *Law of Fiduciaries* (1981), Chaps. 8 and 24.

[59] *Cf.* the duty of a fiduciary agent to disclose all material facts to his principal before engaging in a transaction with him: *De Bussche* v. *Alt* (1877) 8 Ch.D. 286; Goff and Jones, at pp. 637–640.

[60] *Bentley* v. *Craven* (1853) 18 Beav. 75; Partnership Act 1890, ss.29, 30.

[61] *Hospital Products Ltd.* v. *U.S. Surgical Corp.* (1984) 156 C.L.R. 41, 58

A.L.J.R. 587 (H.C.A.). See also *Jewson & Sons* v. *Arcos Ltd.* (1932) 39 Com.Cas. 59, at p. 67 (contract for the sale of goods).
    [62] See Spencer Bower and Turner, *Estoppel By Representation* (3rd ed., 1977), at p. 61. Estoppel by negligence is, however, slightly different: see *ibid.*, p. 72.
    [63] *Ramsden* v. *Dyson* (1866) L.R. 1 H.L. 129 at p. 140, *per* Lord Cranworth L.C.
    [64] *Spiro* v. *Lintern* [1973] 1 W.L.R. 1002 at p. 1011, *per* Buckley L.J.
    [65] Spencer Bower, *Actionable Non-Disclosure*, at para. 157.
    [66] See the authorities cited *supra*, in n. 4.
    [67] *Bates* v. *Hewitt* (1867) L.R. 2 Q.B. 595.
    [68] *Godfrey* v. *Britannic Assurance Co.* [1963] 2 Lloyd's Rep. 515.
    [69] This is the rule for marine insurance (M.I.A., s.18), and should apply generally: *C.T.I.* v. *Oceanus* [1984] 1 Lloyd's Rep. 476.
    [70] See, *e.g. Willmott* v. *Barber* (1880) 15 Ch.D. 96, affmd. (1881) 17 Ch.D. 772.
    [71] See the cases cited *supra* in nn. 67–69. But *cf. Joel* v. *Law Union & Crown Insurance Co.* [1908] 2 K.B. 864, especially *per* Fletcher Moulton L.J. at p. 884.
    [72] See, *e.g. Paterson Zochonis & Co. Ltd.* v. *Merfarken Packaging Ltd.* [1986] 3 All E.R. 522, at pp. 540–541.
    [73] *Supra,* n. 43.
    [74] See, *e.g. Woodward* v. *Row* (1666) 2 Keb. 132; *Williams* v. *Williams* (1693) Carth. 269, and Goode, at pp. 31–35.
    [75] *Gordon* v. *Gordon* (1821) 3 Swan. 400.
    [76] *New Brunswick & Canada Railway Co.* v. *Muggeridge* (1860) 1 Dr. & Sm. 363 at p. 381; *Central Railway of Venezuela* v. *Kisch* (1867) L.R. 2 H.L. 99 at p. 113. See now the requirements set out in the Companies Act 1985, Part III.
    [77] Gilmore, *The Death of Contract* (1974).
    [78] *Cf.* Atiyah, *The Rise and Fall of Freedom of Contract* (1979).
    [79] Goff and Jones; Birks, *An Introduction to the Law of Restitution* (1985).
    [80] See *Blackburn Low* v. *Vigors, supra*, n. 25.
    [81] Colinvaux, para. 5.01; Birds, at p. 83; Halsbury, paras. 366, 378; Chitty, vol. 2, para. 3684; Arnould, *Marine Insurance* (16th ed., 1981) ("Arnould"), para. 627; Welford and Offer-Barker, *Fire Insurance* (3rd ed., 1932), at p. 127.
    [82] (1766) 3 Burr. 1905 at p. 1909.
    [83] *Ibid.*
    [84] *E.g. Re Bradley and Essex and Suffolk Accident Indemnity Society* [1912] 1 K.B. 415 at p. 530; *Goldschlager* v. *Royal Insurance Co.* (1978) 84 D.L.R. (3d) 355.
    [85] *Supra*, n. 43.
    [86] S.17.
    [87] [1987] 1 Lloyd's Rep. 69, 93.
    [88] *Ibid.* at p. 93.
    [89] (1766) 3 Burr. 1905 at 1909. See also *Seaton* v. *Heath* [1899] 1 Q.B. 782.
    [90] *Re Bradley and Essex and Suffolk Accident Indemnity Society, supra*, n. 84.
    [91] *Goulstone* v. *Royal Insurance* (1858) 1 F. & F. 276; *Norton* v. *Royal Insurance* (1885) 1 T.L.R. 460.
    [92] *E.g.* through his agent: *Woolcott* v. *Excess Insurance Co.* [1979] 1 Lloyd's Rep. 231; [1979] 2 Lloyd's Rep. 210. See also M.I.A., s.18(3)(*b*).
    [93] *Re Yager and the Guardian Assurance Co.* (1912) 108 L.T. 38.
    [94] *Lambert* v. *Co-Operative Insurance Services, supra*, n. 2.
    [95] *Carter* v. *Boehm* (1766) 3 Burr. 1905 at p. 1911; M.I.A., s.18(3)(*a*).
    [96] *McCormick* v. *National Motor Accident Insurance Union Ltd.* (1934) 49 Lloyd's Rep. 361 at p.363; M.I.A., s.18(3)(*c*).
    [97] *Lambert* v. *C.I.S., supra*, n. 2.

[98] C.T.I. v. Oceanus [1984] 1 Lloyd's Rep. 476.
[99] C.T.I. v. Oceanus, supra; see Brooke [1985] 4 L.M.C.L.Q. 437; Khan [1986] J.B.L. 37.
[1] Highlands Insurance Co. v. The Continental Insurance Co., [1987] 1 Lloyd's Rep. 109.
[2] [1987] 1 Lloyd's Rep. 69 at p. 94.
[3] Ibid.
[4] Carter v. Boehm (1766) 3 Burr. 1906.
[5] Locker & Woolf v. Western Australian Insurance Co. [1936] 1 K.B. 408 at p. 415; Joel v. Law Union & Crown Insurance Co. [1908] 2 K.B. 863 at p. 884.
[6] MacKender v. Feldia A.G. [1967] 2 Q.B. 590.
[7] Kennedy v. Panama (1867) L.R. 2 Q.B. 580.
[8] Redgrave v. Hurd (1881) 20 Ch.D. 1.
[9] Court v. Martineau (1782) 3 Dougl. 161.
[10] Anderson v. Thornton (1853) 8 Ex. 425; M.I.A., s.84(1), (3)(a).
[11] (1766) 3 Burr. 1905 at p. 1909.
[12] Redgrave v. Hurd, supra, n. 8.
[13] Tyrie v. Fletcher (1777) 2 Cowp. 666 at p. 668; MacGillivray and Parkington, para. 634.
[14] [1908] 1 K.B. 545.
[15] (1937) 57 Lloyd's Rep. 254.
[16] Hedley Byrne v. Heller & Co. [1964] A.C. 465.
[17] Misrepresentation Act 1967, s.2(1).
[18] Jones v. Bowden (1813) 4 Taunt. 847; Wilson v. Fuller (1843) 3 Q.B. 68; Re South of England Natural Gas Co. [1911] 1 Ch. 573; The Odenfeld [1978] 2 Lloyd's Rep. 357 at pp. 377–378; Hurley v. Dyke [1979] R.T.R. 265; The Zinnia [1984] 2 Lloyd's Rep. 211 at p. 218.
[19] The Henrik Sif [1982] 1 Lloyd's Rep. 456; The Lutetia [1982] 2 Lloyd's Rep. 140 at pp. 157–158.
[20] See Leon v. Casey [1932] 2 K.B. 576 at p. 579, and The Litsion Pride [1985] 1 Lloyd's Rep. 437 at pp. 509–511. See Arnould, paras. 1347–1349.
[21] Harding v. Bussell [1905] 2 K.B. 83 at p. 85.
[22] The Chancery Amendment Act 1858 (21 and 22 Vict. c. 27). See now the Supreme Court Act 1981, s.50.
[23] Supra, n. 43.
[24] Ibid. at p. 102.
[25] Except where the obligation being enforced by the court was itself one to pay money: Moschi v. Lep Air Services [1973] A.C. 331 at p. 347 per Lord Diplock.
[26] C.T.I. v. Oceanus [1984] 1 Lloyd's Rep. 476 at pp. 496, 525.
[27] S.18.
[28] See those cited supra in n. 33.
[29] Post, text to n. 31.
[30] Kettlewell v. Refuge Assurance, supra, n. 14; cf. M.I.A., s.20.
[31] S.91(2).
[32] As Chalmers did in the Sale of Goods Act 1893, when he categorised all contractual terms as either conditions or warranties, and failed to recognise the existence of the innominate term: Hong Kong Fir Shipping Co. v. Kawasaki Kaisen Kaisha [1962] 2 Q.B. 26.
[33] (1911) 16 Com.Cas. 109.
[34] Ibid. at p. 121.
[35] [1987] 1 Lloyd's Rep. 69.
[36] Ibid. at p. 96.

[37] *Ibid.* at p. 96.
[38] *Ibid.* at p. 96.
[39] *Cf. JEB Fasteners* v. *Marks Bloom & Co.* [1983] 1 All E.R. 583.
[40] [1987] 1 Lloyd's Rep. 69 at p. 96.

The Proper Law of Insurance and Reinsurance Contracts

ROBERT MERKIN

A. *The Significance of the Proper Law*

The determination by the English courts of the proper law[1] of an insurance or reinsurance agreement has traditionally been an important matter for two purposes, one substantive and one procedural. The substantive purpose is that an English court will apply the proper law of an agreement, whether that law is English law or the law of some other jurisdiction, to all aspects of the formation, construction and consensual discharge of the agreement to which the dispute relates.[2]

In most cases in the context of commercial insurance and reinsurance, determining the proper law will not give rise to much difficulty. There will frequently be an express choice of law clause, which, in the English conflict of laws[3] is to all intents and purposes conclusive evidence of the intention of the parties, irrespective of any lack of connection between the agreement and the legal system nominated.[4] Alternatively, in the absence of any express choice of law, the objective intentions of the parties as to the proper law may be readily (although not conclusively) inferred from, *inter alia*, a clause conferring exclusive jurisdiction to determine disputes on the courts of a specified nation,[5] a clause which fixes the seat of arbitration,[6] a clause which indicates that disputes are to be resolved consistently with those arising under another, associated, agreement which does contain an express choice of law clause,[7] or a clause which refers to or incorporates principles laid down by a specific legal system.[8] Consequently, it is only in rare cases that disputes as to substantive rights under opposing legal systems will arise, and in many of those the question will be one for arbitrators whose decisions are for all practical purposes beyond the powers of review of the English courts.[9]

The procedural significance of the proper law in the insurance and reinsurance context is that English courts have the power to hear an action involving a defendant outside the jurisdiction only where it is possible to serve notice of proceedings on that defendant. The various grounds on which the English courts may give leave for service outside the jurisdiction are contained in R.S.C. Ord. 11, r. 1(1),[10] the most important of which for present purposes is r. 1(1)(f), which permits the exercise of the "exorbitant" jurisdiction where the dispute between the parties relates to a contract the proper law of which is English law. However, it may be that this aspect of the determination of the proper law is also diminishing in importance for, even where one of the grounds in R.S.C. Ord. 11 r. 1(1) has been made out, it remains necessary for the court to be convinced that the case is a proper one in which leave should be given, and recent authority on this matter indicates that the proper law is but one element in the exercise of judicial discretion. The landmark decision on this point is that of the House of Lords in *Amin Rasheed Shipping Corp.* v. *Kuwait Insurance Co.*,[11] in which the leading speech was given by Lord Diplock. He made it clear that leave should not be given for service outside the jurisdiction solely on the basis that the contract is governed by English law, and that the crucial issue is to determine where, taking into account *inter alia* the availability of witnesses and evidence, the action could most conveniently be heard. *Amin Rasheed* is also significant for denouncing the previous trend of the English courts in adopting the view that English procedures are in some way superior to those operated in other jurisdictions, so that leave for service outside the jurisdiction ought generally to be given. After *Amin Rasheed*, it is clear that judicial chauvinism has given way to the desire for international comity.[12]

It may be seen, therefore, that questions which arise in the determination of the proper law of an insurance or reinsurance agreement, and indeed the proper law itself, are of less significance than once was the case as the result of modern trends in insurance and reinsurance practice and of the accommodating attitude of the English courts to the merits of foreign proceedings.

Nevertheless, there are two aspects of the proper law which have recently exercised the English courts, and of which undoubtedly the last has not been heard. First, how can the proper law be determined where the parties have failed to give any convincing indication in the agreement itself? Secondly, in the reinsurance context, how can the courts deal with the problem that reinsurance agreements and their underlying insurances are often governed by different proper laws, with the common consequence that the application of different canons of construction or legal interpretations leaves the reinsured with liabilities not matched by the reinsurance. The remainder of this paper will be devoted to these matters.

B. *Determining the Proper Law of Insurance and Reinsurance Contracts*

1. *The context of the problem*

There is no easy answer in any case to the question, "what is the proper law of an insurance or reinsurance contract?" Indeed, the very fact that the question has to be posed presupposes an international contract brought into existence by a series of supplementary national and transnational dealings. Consider, to take a much simplified illustration, a French entrepreneur who wishes to insure a subject-matter or liability of sufficient magnitude to merit international coverage. The assured's brokers in France are asked to place the risk, and they in turn contact London brokers, instructing them to arrange insurance on the London market, the London brokers thereafter obtaining cover from an English insurer. The assured has some justification for arguing that the proper law of the ultimate insurance ought to be that of France, as the risks or liabilities insured against are those defined or imposed by French canons of construction and accepted by the insurer. However, the insurer may counter, with equal plausibility, that the premium received by it was based upon an English law interpretation of the coverage granted and that the assured, by opting for an English insurer, must also impliedly have opted for English law. Even if it were possible to justify satisfactorily a value judgment between these opposing arguments, the adopted solution could scarcely survive the practical realities of international insurance arrangements. There may be more than one proposer for cover and, consequently, more than one domestic law on the assured's side of the equation; this is particularly common where facultative reinsurance is sought by a number of reinsureds in relation to a particular risk. However, by the same token there may well be a number of insurers of different nationalities, each taking a given percentage of the risk, and in those circumstances the assured potentially faces differing proper laws governing his insurance cover. Where a number of assureds of differing nationalities are insured by a number of insurers of differing nationalities, any suggestion that the proper law is to be determined by the head office of either the assured or the insurer simply cannot be applied, and any solution based on the head office of the leading underwriter or of the representative assured smacks of arbitrariness.

This analysis suggests that the solution is to be found by reference to criteria which are independent of the domiciles or residences of the parties. Four possibilities suggest themselves here.

The first is the law of the place in which the contract was entered into. The problem with this approach is that "in these days of modern methods of communication where international contracts are so frequently negotiated by telex, whether what turns out to be the final offer is accepted in the country where one telex is situated or in the country where the other telex is installed is often a matter of mere chance."[13] The *lex loci contractus* may thus safely be disregarded. Secondly, there is the law of the place in which the policy was issued. This, however, depends upon whether a policy is "issued" when it is sent or when it is received, so that the dispute as to competing domiciles outlined above is taken no further. Thirdly, we have the law of the place of performance. A particular problem arises in the insurance context in considering the *lex loci solutionis*, as performance consists merely of the transfer of sums, whether by way of premium or by way of settlement. Consequently, one is driven back to the currency adopted by the contract, but "very often what is used is an international rather than a national currency."[14] Moreover, in a typical international transaction money (whether in respect of premiums or claims) is transferred to and by the relevant brokers and, as between the broker placing the insurance and the insurer, money will generally change hands only following quarterly accounting settlements and not in respect of individual transactions. The fourth and remaining possibility is the law of the place in which the process of the formation of the agreement primarily took place. It is suggested that, after initial judicial hostility, this solution has now been accepted by the courts as forming a part of English law. It remains to trace the processes by which this took place.

2. *The early English cases*

Dicey and Morris suggests, somewhat tentatively, that the trend of the English cases is in favour of the proper law being provided by the place at which the insurer carries on business or, if the insurer carries on business in more than one place, the location of its head office. This conclusion is justified by *Dicey and Morris* on a practical basis by the fact that life insurances in particular are conditional on head office approval and that insurers' branches, unlike the branches of banks and other financial institutions, are not authorised to commit the head office to long-term risks.[15] The authorities on which this statement is based are, however, both atypical as to their facts and, on occasions, poorly reasoned.

Pick v. *Manufacturers' Life Insurance Co.*[16] and *Rossano* v. *Manufacturers' Life Insurance Co.*[17] concerned assureds, domiciled in Palestine and Egypt respectively, who had taken out life policies with the Egyptian branch of an insurer which had its head office in Ontario. In both cases the law of Ontario was held to be the proper law, and there are clear indications in the judgments that the location of the insurer's head office was of some significance to these results. Insofar as the decisions involve a balancing exercise between the competing systems of law to see with which the agreements had the closest connection, they cannot be faulted. But McNair J.'s assumption in *Rossano*, that an assured who chooses to insure with a particular insurer must be taken to have assented to the application of the proper law of the jurisdiction in which that insurer has its head office, bears little resemblance to reality, particularly in the life context.[18] Whatever the role of the insurer's head office principle in non-indemnity insurance, the authority for the same approach in indemnity insurance is less convincing. *Greer* v. *Poole*,[19] cited by *Dicey and Morris* in support of the head office rule in the context of indemnity insurance, is admittedly in its result entirely consistent with that principle, but the marine cargo policy in question was negotiated and entered into in England by British subjects and was in standard English form; the only element of the agreement not connected with England was the fact that the insured cargo was to be carried on board a French ship. It is, therefore, hardly surprising, that Lush J. gave short shrift to the argument that the proper law was not English law but French law.

An important indication that the head office principle is not of significance in indemnity insurance is provided by reinsurance authority, reinsurance of course being perhaps the most important form of indemnity insurance against liability. *Dicey and Morris*, without elaboration, simply notes that reinsurance agreements may be governed by different rules.[20] Indeed, there has been some suggestion that the proper law of a reinsurance agreement is determined by the head office of the reinsured.[21] This approach is based on a general acceptance of the head office rule, but its reversal in reinsurance cases is said to be justified on the grounds that the reinsured frequently settles the terms of the contract and that it is important to the reinsured that its reinsurance arrangements are governed by a single proper law where cover has been obtained from reinsurers in a number of different jurisdictions. It is nevertheless suggested by the present writer that this view is misguided. In the first place, neither of these points is persuasive: as to the former, in practice, the terms of reinsurance agreements are prepared for the most part by the reinsurer's brokers, although in a limited number of cases this task may be undertaken by the reinsured or by the reinsurer; and the latter disregards the problems faced by a reinsurer who has agreed to indemnify in relation to the same risk a number of reinsureds domiciled in different jurisdictions.[22] Secondly, there is no early reinsurance case which turns on the head office of either party. On the contrary, the only case prior to the 1970s in which the proper law of a reinsurance agreement has called for decision, *Royal Exchange Assurance Corp.* v. *Vega*,[23] concerned a jurisdiction clause which was regarded by at least two members of the Court of Appeal as conclusive, and which strongly influenced the third.

3. The modern trend

(a) *Moves towards a new approach.* It is clear from the above that the early English cases are of little assistance: other than in the rather special context of life insurance, they are not conclusive; and they do not remotely deal with the modern situation in which there may be a multiplicity of parties as assureds/reinsureds and insurers/reinsurers. The way forward appears first to have been suggested by Bingham J. in *Royal Exchange Assurance Corp.* v. *Vega*.[24] As noted above, the Court of Appeal was content to rest its decision on the presence of a jurisdiction clause. But, in opting for English law as the proper law, the trial judge considered a variety of other matters, including the facts that the terms of the agreement had been arranged in London and that it was in standard Lloyd's form. There is here, then, an early indication that the machinery by which an international transaction comes into being is of some significance. Support for such a proposition is to be found in *Armadora Occidental S.A.* v. *Horace Mann Insurance Co.*[25] This case concerned insurances, issued by insurers in the United States, England, Japan, Belgium and Greece, on 29 vessels owned by various Panamanian and Liberian companies. The cover was obtained by brokers in San Francisco operating on the San Francisco market. Kerr J. and the Court of Appeal held that, had the intentions of the parties to have the agreements governed by English law not been clearly manifested in a "follow London" clause, the law with which the agreements had their closest connection was that operative in San Francisco.

The "machinery" approach received the full approval of the Court of Appeal soon afterwards in *Citadel Insurance Co.* v. *Atlantic Union Insurance Co. S.A.*[26] This case concerned facultative reinsurances placed with a Greek reinsurer by a Canadian reinsured. The reinsured had approached American brokers, who had in turn contacted London brokers. The London brokers sought

and obtained an open cover from the reinsurers, and thereafter
individual risks were accepted under the open cover by slips prepared in London and initialled in London by the reinsurers' London agents. Bingham J. at first instance ruled that he did not have
jurisdiction to give leave for service outside the jurisdiction as the
proper law of the reinsurance agreements was not English law: in
the view of the learned judge, the contract had no substantial connection with the English system of law, and England had been
used as a forum for the transaction merely for the sake of conve-
nience. This conclusion was, however, vigorously rejected by Kerr
L.J., Oliver L.J. concurring, in the Court of Appeal. What
Bingham J. had regarded as mere mechanisms were, according to
Kerr L.J., the very substance of the transaction:

> "The whole point of the business, both from the point of view
> of the defendants as reinsurers and of the reinsured plaintiffs,
> was run . . . in London. All the documents are here, and it is
> only by an examination of those documents that it is possible
> to determine the rights and wrongs of the dispute."[27]

The judgment of Kerr L.J. is also of importance for his use of
the phrase "centre of gravity" to describe the legal system with
which an insurance contract has its closest connection. Although it
is probably the case that Kerr L.J. did not attach any great significance to his choice of wording, it has subsequently come to be
adopted as an acronym for the place in which the machinery for
setting the contract in motion was located.

(b) *A possible reversal.* However, the general adoption of the
law of the place in which an international insurance agreement was
formed as the proper law received a setback in the litigation in the
Amin Rasheed case.[28] The main question facing the Court of
Appeal and the House of Lords was whether the proper law of a
marine policy on the *Al Wahab*, issued by a Kuwaiti insurer to
Liberian owners, issued originally in 1977 and thereafter renewed
twice, could be Kuwaiti law, given that Kuwait did not at the date
of the second renewal of the policy have any marine insurance law
of its own. The fact that the policy was in the then standard English form contained in Schedule 1 of the Marine Insurance Act
1906, coupled with the lack of a Kuwaiti marine insurance law, was
enough to convince the majority of the Court of Appeal, Robert
Goff L.J. dissenting, and the entire House of Lords, Lord Wilberforce *dubitante*, that English law was the proper law of the policy,
on the basis that the 1906 Act alone supplied the definitions and
rules by which sense could be made of the Lloyd's S.G. policy

employed.[29] Leaving aside these rather exceptional facts of the case, it is of some interest for its potential impact on the "centre of gravity" approach.

It was argued in the Court of Appeal that the centre of gravity of the contract was England. This was on the strength of a number of factors: the policy was entirely administered in England; premiums were paid in sterling by the plaintiff to its London brokers; all claims and settlements were dealt with in London by the brokers; the dealings between the brokers and the insurer were by way of running account with periodic settlements; and the insurer's liability had been reinsured on the London market. It might be thought that these factors would, on a *Citadel* v. *Atlantic*[30] approach, have concluded the question of the proper law in favour of English law. However, in the Court of Appeal, Sir John Donaldson M.R. carefully pointed out that the involvement of the brokers had come about some time in 1978, after the formation of the 1977 policy, and that the brokers in question had originally been the insurer's own brokers for reinsurance purposes. Consequently, adopting the view that the renewals were merely extensions of the original policy, and the principle that conduct subsequent to the formation of a contract cannot be used to construe the intentions of the parties on formation, Donaldson M.R. concluded that the factors allegedly connecting the policy with English law were of no weight and that the "centre of gravity" argument had no application. This way of looking at the case was approved by May L.J., Robert Goff L.J. not commenting on the point. It is clear, therefore, that those members of the Court of Appeal who considered the machinery argument, dismissed it only on the rather unusual facts of the case. This is not, however, made fully clear in a passage from the judgment on appeal of Lord Wilberforce, who, alone in the House of Lords considered the factors dismissed by the Court of Appeal. Lord Wilberforce expressed himself in these words[31]:

> "I agree with [Sir John Donaldson M.R.] that the majority of the ingredients said to connect the policy with English law are irrelevant or lacking in weight: these include . . . the use of . . . London brokers."

This passage is clearly open to the interpretation that such a factor is always irrelevant, and it is suggested that what was intended here was an expression of agreement with Donaldson M.R.'s *reasons* for regarding those factors as irrelevant.

On the assumption that *Amin Rasheed* is to be regarded as exceptional in that the machinery was not established until after the formation of the contract, two practical difficulties arise. The first is the assumption of Donaldson M.R. that renewal policies are simply to be regarded as continuations of an original policy. While this may be true in some situations, it is often the case that renewal provides an important opportunity for renegotiation; this is particularly so where treaty reinsurances are involved, treaties generally containing provisions terminating the legal relationship of the parties and requiring what in effect amounts to a new agreement to reactivate its provisions. It may be that in *Amin Rasheed* the intervention of the brokers did not result in renegotiation before either of the renewals; but it should be clear that, had such renegotiation taken place, Donaldson M.R.'s reasoning would have been without foundation. The second difficulty is that *Amin Rasheed* draws a clear distinction between machinery on formation, which does influence the proper law, and machinery in the administration of a policy, which may not. This would appear not only to be inconsistent with the tenor of the judgment of Kerr L.J. in *Citadel* v. *Atlantic*, but also difficult to apply: in determining the proper law, is a court to disregard, for example, an express term in an insurance agreement which provides for its post-formation administration within a specified jurisdiction? *Amin Rasheed* may well be good law only on the basis that the policy did not contemplate London administration, and that the appointment of brokers was an afterthought; if this is correct, then it would appear that *Amin Rasheed* is truly an exceptional decision.

(c) *Reaffirmation.* There have been a number of significant cases involving insurance in the wake of *Amin Rasheed*, all of which demonstrate a strengthening of the move towards the mechanics of creation test adopted in *Citadel* v. *Atlantic*. Two examples will suffice. In *Afia Worldwide Insurance Co.* v. *Deutsche Ruck Versicherungs A.G.*,[32] 64 reinsurance agreements had been entered into by a number of English ceding companies with three reinsurers, two in West Germany and one in Italy. The reinsurers had appointed I.C.R.A. as its agent in Holland, with authority to enter into reinsurance agreements, and I.C.R.A. had in turn appointed a London agent, F.R.A., to receive proposals for reinsurance from London brokers, to negotiate terms and to submit the proposals to I.C.R.A. A number of the agreements contained arbitration clauses nominating London as the seat of arbitration, and Mustill J. was able to hold without too much difficulty that in those instances English law had been intended to be the proper law. A significant number of the agreements did not contain such clauses, but Mustill J. nevertheless reached the same conclusion as to the proper law, by giving particular weight to a number of factors: all negotiations had been conducted in London between the reinsureds' brokers and F.R.A., I.C.R.A. in Holland merely confirming the resulting agreements on behalf of the reinsurers; the slips had been prepared by the reinsureds' brokers in London, using standard London forms; and it could be presumed that the intention of the various parties was that the payment of premiums and the settlement of claims should occur in London (which had indeed proved to be the case). Two points are noteworthy here. First, Mustill J. gave no weight to the coincidental fact that the reinsureds' head offices were in England, and it is clear from the reasoning adopted that English law would have been the proper law of the agreements irrespective of the location of the contracting parties. Secondly, Mustill J. did not distinguish the post-formation administration of the policies: indeed, he was prepared to assume, in the absence of evidence to the contrary, that the pre-contractual intention of the parties had been to that effect and that it was a matter of some weight. Where brokers are used in the formation process it would appear perfectly proper, as a matter of practicality, to assume that subsequent administration is to be left in their hands, and it is consequently possible to confine the *Amin Rasheed* reasoning to the limited number of cases in which either brokers are not used in the process or formation or are intended to be used for that purpose only.

Again, in *Cantieri Navali Riuniti S.p.A.* v. *N.V. Omne Justitia (The Stolt Marmaro)*[33] the Court of Appeal was faced with a series of marine policies issued to American owners by 44 insurers with head offices throughout the world, many of the insurers executing their own policies within their own particular jurisdictions. It was clearly impossible in this type of case to apply the head office principle, even had the Court of Appeal wished to do so, and the dispute crystallised into one between American law and English law. In favour of the former were the factors that the American Institute Hull Clauses had been appended to the policies, and that the policies contained a permissive "New York suable" clause. In favour of English law were the usual machinery arguments: the policies had been arranged in London by English brokers using standard London market broking slips; and the policies were in the (now defunct[34]) Lloyd's S.G. form. In opting for English law on "centre of gravity" grounds, the Court of Appeal appears finally to have established that the formative process of an insurance or reinsurance agreement is now, in the absence of arbitration, jurisdiction, choice of law and other similar clauses, the most important factor in determining its proper law. Given the predominance of the London market in insurance and reinsurance matters, this is clearly good news for London lawyers; but, given the nature of, and multiplicity of parties to, international agreements, it is difficult to see what other approach could sensibly be adopted.

C. *Harmonising Insurance and Reinsurance Cover Through the Proper Law*

1. *Outline of the problem*

It is unlikely to be the case that any two legal systems operate precisely the same insurance laws. Consequently, important matters such as the legal meaning of words, the canons of construction adopted and the consequences of a breach of duty, condition or warranty, will vary as between jurisdictions. This is clearly a serious problem in the reinsurance context. The original insurance may be governed by proper law generous to the assured, while the reinsurance agreement may be governed by a proper law more responsive to the needs of (re)insurers: as a consequence, the same words in the insurance and reinsurance agreements may impose liability upon the reinsured in one jurisdiction but exempt the reinsurer from liability in the other.[35] As a result, the legitimate expectation of the reinsured that its liability was matched by the liability of the reinsurer may be defeated. In order to ascertain the extent of this potential difficulty, it is necessary to distinguish between two of the forms that a reinsurance agreement may take: that which defines the reinsurer's liability independently in a formal policy; and that which simply obliges the reinsurer to indemnify the reinsured against its liability under one or more original policies.

The former class of policy raises squarely the problem of conflicting proper laws, and the English courts have shown no inclination to resolve it. In *St. Paul Fire and Marine Insurance Co.* v. *Morice*,[36] a marine policy, governed by New York law, was issued against the "mortality" of a bull. The American insurer effected reinsurance at Lloyd's under a policy governed by English law, one of the stated risks being "mortality." The bull was destroyed while still on board the vessel, as a result of its having been in contact with foot and mouth disease. The insurers paid the loss, as they were obliged to do in the light of the meaning of "mortality" in New York law, but Kennedy J. ruled that their action on the reinsurance policy had to fail, as the definition of "mortality" in English law was not wide enough to encompass the circumstances that had occurred.

The second class of case is that in which the reinsurer simply agrees to indemnify the reinsured against liability, the original policy being appended to the reinsurance slip. The usual form of wording used on the London market for this purpose has become known as the "full reinsurance clause," and runs "being a reinsurance of and warranted same gross rate and terms and conditions and to follow the settlements."[37] In theory no difficulty in matching the coverage of the original insurance and the reinsurance arises under this clause, as the reinsurer's liability is defined in terms only of the reinsured's liability under the proper law of its original insurance. However, the position has become somewhat complicated by the development of the notion in English law that the phrase "warranted same gross rate and terms and conditions" serves to import into the reinsurance agreement the wording of the original insurance, thereby creating a possible conflict in proper laws not contemplated by the reinsurance agreement itself. The problem is highlighted by the recent decision of Hobhouse J. in *Vesta* v. *Butcher*,[38] which will be considered following an outline of the history and nature of the full reinsurance clause.

2. *The Full Reinsurance Clause*

This clause falls into two distinct parts, the first consisting of the warranty as to gross rate and terms and conditions, and the second amounting to a promise by the reinsurer to follow the reinsured's settlements. The use of the first part of the clause appears to have originated late in the nineteenth century, in the form of a stamping on or addition to a standard form original insurance policy, the objects being to make it clear that the policy was one of reinsurance and to facilitate the grant of facultative cover in those frequent cases in which a copy of the original policy was not available.[39] However, almost immediately the phrase was taken by the courts to be effective to incorporate into the reinsurance agreement the terms of the original policy. This inevitably caused problems where the terms of the original insurance were either inappropriate to, or in direct conflict with, the terms of the reinsurance agreement. Consequently, the courts were forced to fashion the general principle that incorporation was possible only where appropriate and non-conflicting. As a result, formal requirements in original policies, particularly notice provisions, were not to be regarded as incorporated,[40] attempts to extend the express coverage of a reinsurance agreement to the wider coverage granted by the original insurance were rejected,[41] and increases of the original risk not initially contemplated but accepted by the reinsured were held not to be covered by the reinsurance.[42] By this complex process, the courts came to confer upon the phrase its intended meaning, namely that the reinsurer thereby agreed to indemnify the reinsured against liability, subject to any retention level and to any financial or event limits; the terms of the original policy were not to be incorporated to alter this fundamental obligation.

The second element of the clause, the agreement of the reinsurer to follow the reinsured's settlements, may be traced back to the first quarter of the present century. Its purpose was to avoid the need for the reinsured to prove its loss (*i.e.* for the reinsured to demonstrate that it had paid or settled with the assured on the basis of legal liability alone) and to allow the reinsured to recover for liability incurred under a bona fide and businesslike settlement with the reinsured even though it might later be proved that the reinsured was not under any legal liability. This form of wording was adopted once it had become clear that an earlier form of wording employed for the same purpose—"to pay as may be paid thereon"—did not achieve its purpose and allowed indemnity for payments based on legal liability only.[43] The effect of the "follow the settlements" clause was tested for the first time, some fifty years after its adoption, in *Insurance Co. of Africa* v. *Scor (U.K.) Reinsurance Co. Ltd.*,[44] the Court of Appeal holding that the wording did indeed achieve its purpose of obliging the reinsurer to follow bona fide and businesslike settlements whether or not based on the reinsured's legal liability. *Scor* is also significant in establishing that, where a "follow the settlements" clause is to be found in conjunction with a claims co-operation or claims control clause (whereby the reinsurer is not to be bound by a settlement to which it has not consented or is authorised to take over all negotiations with the assured from the reinsured), the latter is to take precedence and in practical terms deprives the former of all effect. The practice of including a claims co-operation or claims control clause is not, however, universal, and its sole purpose is to protect the reinsurer against the settlements of a reinsured of which the reinsurer has little or no knowledge.[45]

The purpose of this brief analysis is to demonstrate that the full reinsurance clause, far from contemplating the creation of difficulties by incorporation, has the opposite objective of imposing liability upon the reinsurer whenever the reinsured reaches a bona fide and businesslike settlement with the assured under the original policy and in accordance with the proper law of that policy. The proper law of the insurance contract is, as will be appreciated, irrelevant to the basic obligation of the reinsurer to indemnify the reinsured for properly obtained settlements.

3. *Vesta* v. *Butcher*[46]

(a) *Facts and assumptions of law.* The plaintiff in this case was the Norwegian insurer of a fish farm located in Norway and insured under a policy governed by Norwegian law. The policy contained three clauses of particular importance: a claims control clause, under which the insurers reserved to themselves the exclusive right to control any proceedings brought against the assured by third parties; a stock control clause, which obliged the assured to maintain regular stock records; and a warranty by the assured that a 24 hour watch would be kept over the insured premises. Vesta reinsured its liability at Lloyd's, in the form of a slip containing the full reinsurance clause and to which were appended the most important clauses contained in the original policy. By all normal criteria the reinsurance contract was governed by English law. Following a loss under the original policy, Vesta reached a settlement with the assured, and then sought indemnity under the reinsurance contract. The defendants raised three defences to Vesta's action on that agreement: Vesta had reached a settlement with the assured in breach of the claims control clause; the original assured had failed to keep proper accounting records; and the original assured had not maintained a proper watch over the premises.

The fundamental assumption underlying each of these defences was that the terms of the original insurance had been incorporated into the reinsurance agreement, and this indeed was accepted to be the case by Hobhouse J. This conclusion is at first sight understandable, given the fact that the original policy was annexed to the reinsurance slip, but further reflection makes it perfectly plain that the assumption as to incorporation was entirely erroneous. In the first place, the original policy and the reinsurance agreement were to an extent in conflict. *Scor*[47] established that claims control and full reinsurance clauses within the same agreement pull in opposite directions and that their reconciliation required the subversion of the latter to the former: by assuming incorporation, Hobhouse J. almost eliminated the express duty of the reinsurers to follow Vesta's settlements and replaced it with an incorporated obligation on Vesta not to settle but to pass control of negotiations with the original assured to the reinsurers. The creation of inconsistency by incorporation is, as previously noted, contrary to authority. It might also be pointed out that the claims control clause in the original policy presumably related to third party claims against the assured, a context entirely different to the circumstances of the actual loss. Secondly, the incorporation of the stock control and watch clauses into the reinsurance agreement makes little sense. Those obligations were imposed by Vesta on the assured under the original policy; compliance with them and the effect of any breach of them was a matter for Norwegian law only. Treating those clauses as incorporated into the reinsurance agreement made it necessary for Vesta to demonstrate that, under the proper law of the reinsurance contract, either the clauses had not been infringed or any infringements did not or would not permit a repudiation of liability. Incorporation in these circumstances thus inserted into the reinsurance agreement a double burden on Vesta: the need to prove its liability not just under Norwegian law but also under the proper law of the reinsurance contract.

(b) *The claims control issue.* The concern of the present paper is with the conflict of laws problems raised by incorporation of the stock control and watch clauses, as opposed to the inconsistency created by the incorporation of the claims control clause. However, it is worth noting in passing that Hobhouse J. was able to overcome the reinsurers' argument based on the claims control clause, on the ground that Vesta had been able to prove its loss: by so doing its claim was not based on the full reinsurance clause, and its failure to comply with the claims control clause had not caused any prejudice to the reinsurers. This reasoning closely follows that in *Scor*.[48] It must nevertheless be commented that the majority of claims co-operation and claims control clauses are expressed to be conditions precedent to liability (as was the case in *Scor*), and that, had the clause in the original policy been so expressed, Vesta's claim would have been defeated, irrespective of its ability to prove its loss by establishing legal liability under Norwegian law.

(c) *The stock control and watch clauses issue.* On the facts the stock control clause did not give rise to any difficulty, as the learned judge was satisfied that under both Norwegian law and English law breach of the clause did not permit repudiation of liability. The real problem related to the 24 hour watch clause. Hobhouse J. here concluded that as a matter of Norwegian law the clause did not provide a defence in the circumstances, so that Vesta's settlement under the original policy had been entirely proper. However, Hobhouse J. was equally clear that, as a matter of English law, the fact that the clause was expressed as a warranty would have provided a defence. The problem may thus easily be seen: if the proper law of the reinsurance contract was to be held to be English law, Vesta would be held to be in breach of warranty as a result of the incorporation of the watch clause into the reinsurance agreement, and no claim could be made. Applying ordinary principles of the determination of the proper law would thus have led to the paradoxical situation that a clause originally intended to oblige the reinsurer to follow the bona fide settlements of the reinsured would have had the very opposite effect, that of imposing English law obligations on the reinsured wider than those faced by the original assured.

Hobhouse J.'s solution to this dilemma was ingenious. The learned judge seized upon often quoted but never applied dicta,[49] to the effect that different parts of an agreement may be governed by different proper laws, and held that, although the reinsurance agreement as a whole was governed by English law, the watch clause was intended by the parties to be governed by Norwegian law. By the use of reasoning which was breathtaking in its circularity, Hobhouse J. felt able to discover that intention in the wording of the full reinsurance clause: the clause provided that the terms and conditions of the insurance and reinsurance policies were to be the same, and it followed that any terms defining the scope of the reinsurance cover should be interpreted in the same way as those fixing the scope of the original insurance. Hobhouse J. chose to go further and to express the view that, if this conclusion was unsupportable, he would have been prepared to hold that the proper law of the reinsurance agreement was Norwegian law.

It is readily apparent that Hobhouse J.'s problems here were of his own making. Had he taken the view that the full reinsurance clause did not permit the incorporation of anything in the original insurance inconsistent with, or inappropriate to, the express provisions of the reinsurance contract, the reinsurers' obligation would, as a matter of English law, have remained merely to indemnify the reinsured for its liabilities under Norwegian law. However, by treating the full reinsurance clause as one authorising the incorporation into the reinsurance contract of the original insurance contract, it became necessary for Hobhouse J. to rely on the selfsame clause to relieve himself of the difficulty of non-matching cover created by its original misapplication. It might be argued that no real harm was done on the facts of the case, as the undoubtedly correct result was reached, albeit by tortuous reasoning. However, matters may not always be that simple. Suppose, for example, that the reinsurance agreement had expressly provided that it was to be governed by English law. In those circumstances Hobhouse J. could have given effect to the intention of the parties only by denying the validity, in whole or in part, of their expressed intention as to the proper law, and it is by no means clear that such an approach would have been open to him in the present state of the English authorities.[50]

D. *Concluding Comments*

The above discussion is intended to demonstrate that, on a proper analysis, there is no real difficulty created by the typical reinsurance contract, under which a slip containing a full reinsurance clause has appended to it the original policy. As long as it is remembered that there are two agreements, each governed by its own proper law, confusion should be avoided. Problems will arise, as previously mentioned, where insurance and reinsurance agreements subject to differing proper laws seek to define the scope of their respective coverages, whether or not the same words are used in those policies. The solution here is the prudent adoption of express choice of law clauses.

Notes

[1] Defined by Dicey and Morris, *The Conflict of Laws* (10th ed., 1980), at p. 747, as "the system of law by which the parties intended the contract to be governed, or, where their intention is neither expressed nor to be inferred from the circumstances, the system of law with which the transaction has its closest and most real connection."

[2] On the role of the proper law in matters of contract, see *Dicey and Morris, op. cit.*, Chap. 28.

[3] *Vita Food Products Inc.* v. *Unus Shipping Co. Ltd.* [1939] A.C. 277 postulates exceptional cases in which an express choice of law clause could be overriden if its operation were contrary to public policy, although there is no English case in which such a finding has been made.

[4] *Anderson* v. *Equitable Assurance Society of the United States* (1926) 134 L.T. 557.

[5] *Royal Exchange Assurance Corp.* v. *Vega* [1902] 2 K.B. 384, an approach which rendered the agreement in this case void. The weight given to the exclusive jurisdiction clause on such facts would today be regarded as excessive: *Compagnie d'Armement Maritime S.A.* v. *Compagnie Tunisienne de Navigation S.A.* [1971] A.C. 572. Contrast the position in which the jurisdiction clause is permissive or optional rather than mandatory: *Armadora Occidental S.A.* v. *Horace Mann Insurance Co.* [1977] 1 W.L.R. 1098; *Cantieri Navali Riuniti S.p.A.* v. *N.V. Omne Justitia (The Stolt Marmaro)* [1985] 2 Lloyd's Rep. 428 (C.A.).

[6] *Maritime Insurance Co.* v. *Assecuranz Union von 1865* (1935) 52 Ll.L.R. 16, a decision which, like *Royal Exchange* v. *Vega, supra,* cannot survive *Compagnie D'Armement Maritime, supra; Norske Atlas Insurance Co. Ltd.* v. *London General Insurance Co. Ltd.* (1927) 43 T.L.R. 541.

[7] *Armadora Occidental S.A.* v. *Horace Mann Insurance Co.* [1977] 1 W.L.R. 1098, which involved a "follow London" clause. *Cf.* for the same principle *Vesta* v. *Butcher, infra,* n. 46, of which much more will be said below.

[8] *Spurrier* v. *La Cloche* [1902] A.C. 446. But see, *per contra, Ex parte Dever* (1887) 18 Q.B.D. 660.

[9] By virtue of the Arbitration Act 1979. The Act allows the courts to intervene in exceptional cases only and permits the parties to an agreement to exclude, to a greater or lesser degree, the review powers of the courts.

[10] S.I. 1965 No. 1776, recast (without implication for the present analysis) when

R.S.C. (Amendment No. 2) 1983 (S.I. 1983 No. 1181) was brought into force (on January 1, 1987). The complex provisions governing jurisdiction in insurance matters, as between the courts of the member states of the EEC, are outside the scope of this paper.

¹¹ [1984] A.C. 50, an insurance case. For similar reinsurance authority, see *Insurance Co. of Ireland* v. *Strombus International Insurance Co.* [1985] 2 Lloyd's Rep. 138 (C.A.), which illustrates an unsuccessful attempt to remove a dispute from its natural overseas forum by praying in aid English law as the proper law of the agreement.

¹² The *Amin Rasheed* principle has been adopted by the House of Lords in two further and related contexts: the principle of *forum non conveniens*, as it applies to staying English proceedings in favour of more convenient foreign proceedings, in *The Abidin Daver* [1984] A.C. 398 and in *Spiliada Maritime Corporation* v. *Cansulex Ltd.* [1986] 3 W.L.R. 972; Briggs [1987] 1 L.M.C.L.Q. 1; and the notion that advantageous foreign procedural rules may be used to obtain evidence located abroad but required for English proceedings, in *South Carolina Insurance Co.* v. *Assurantie Maatschappij "De Zeven Provincien" N.V.* [1987] A.C. 24.

¹³ *Amin Rasheed* v. *Kuwait Insurance* [1984] A.C. 50, 62, *per* Lord Diplock.

¹⁴ *Ibid. Cf. ibid.*, 71, *per* Lord Wilberforce. See also Donaldson M.R. in the Court of Appeal, [1983] 1 W.L.R. 228, 234–235.

¹⁵ *Dicey and Morris*, *op. cit.*, 862–867: Rule 158(2). *Quaere* whether the branches of banks and similar institutions are so authorised: most, if not all, are subject to financial ceilings.

¹⁶ [1958] 2 Lloyd's Rep. 93.

¹⁷ [1963] 2 Q.B. 352.

¹⁸ On these cases generally, see Unger (1964) 13 I.C.L.Q. 482; and on the head office principle, see Kahn-Freund (1959) 22 M.L.R. 195.

¹⁹ (1880) 5 Q.B.D. 272.

²⁰ *Op. cit.*, 866.

²¹ See Monachos [1972] J.B.L. 206.

²² These and related issues are considered at greater length in Butler and Merkin, *Reinsurance Law* (1986), Chap. D.4.2.

²³ [1902] 2 K.B. 384. Other authorities cited by Dr. Monachos, *loc cit.*, for her proposition are clearly not in point; see Butler and Merkin, *op.cit.*

²⁴ *Supra.*

²⁵ [1977] 1 W.L.R. 1098.

²⁶ [1982] 2 Lloyd's Rep. 543.

²⁷ *Ibid.* at pp. 549–550. The third member of the Court, Lord Denning M.R., gave no reasons for reaching a similar conclusion as to the proper law.

²⁸ [1983] 1 W.L.R. 228, *affd.* [1984] A.C. 50.

²⁹ The Lloyd's S.G. policy is contained in the Marine Insurance Act 1906, Sched. 1. Its use has been superseded by new forms issued by Lloyd's and the Institute of London Underwriters.

³⁰ *Supra*, n. 26.

³¹ [1984] A.C. 50, at p. 71.

³² (1983) 133 N.L.J. 621.

³³ [1985] 2 Lloyd's Rep. 428. See also *E.I. du Pont de Nemours & Co.* v. *Agnew* (1986) unreported; *Islamic Arab Insurance Co.* v. *Saudi Egyptian American Reinsurance Co.*, *The Times*, 26 January, 1987; [1987] 2 C.L. 244.

³⁴ See *supra*, n. 29.

³⁵ Some specific examples are given in Butler and Merkin, *op. cit.* Chap. B.2.1.

³⁶ (1906) 22 T.L.R. 449; 11 Com.Cas. 153.

³⁷ A similar clause was appended to the reinsurance agreement in the *St. Paul*

case, but Kennedy J. gave it little weight. The modern practice is the reverse, *i.e.* to append the original policy to a reinsurance slip containing the full reinsurance clause.

[38] *Forsikringsaktieselskapet Vesta* v. *Butcher* [1986] 2 All E.R. 488.

[39] Butler and Merkin, *op. cit.* Chap. C.1.2.

[40] *Home Insurance Co. of New York* v. *Victoria-Montreal Fire Insurance Co.* [1907] A.C. 59; *Australian Widows Fund Life Assurance Society* v. *National Mutual Life Association of Australasia Ltd.* [1914] A.C. 634. The position is the same in the United States: see *Homan* v. *Employers Reinsurance Corp.* 136 S.W. 2d 289 (1939).

[41] *Franco-Hungarian Insurance Co.* v. *Merchants Marine Insurance Co.*, Shipping Gazette, June 1888: *Maritime Insurance Co.* v. *Stearns* [1901] 1 K.B. 912. Later cases on this point reach the same result but by the rather odd reasoning that incorporation is possible although where its effect is to extend the reinsurer's liability in an unusual fashion the reinsurance agreement is voidable for non-disclosure: see, *e.g. Property Insurance Co. Ltd.* v. *National Protector Insurance Co. Ltd.* (1913) 108 L.T. 104; 12 Asp. M.L.C. 287. The authorities are analysed fully in Butler and Merkin, *op. cit.* Chaps. A.6.4 and B.1.2.

[42] *Lower Rhine and Wurtemburg Insurance Association* v. *Sedgwick* [1899] 1 Q.B. 179; *Norwich Union Fire Insurance Society Ltd.* v. *Colonial Mutual Fire Insurance Co. Ltd.* [1922] 2 K.B. 461; *Scottish National Insurance Co. Ltd.* v. *Poole* (1912) 107 L.T. 687, 12 Asp.M.L.C. 266; *Emanuel & Co.* v. *Andrew Weir & Co.* (1914) 30 T.L.R. 518.

[43] This was established in a series of cases, culminating in *Gurney* v. *Grimmer* (1932) 38 Com.Cas. 7; 44 Ll.L.R. 189. The development is traced in Butler and Merkin, *op. cit.*, Chap. C.1.2.

[44] [1985] 1 Lloyd's Rep. 312; [1986] 2 L.M.C.L.Q. 145.

[45] Butler and Merkin, *op. cit.* Chap. C.4.3.

[46] *Forsikringsaktieselskabet Vesta* v. *Butcher* (henceforth simply *Vesta* v. *Butcher*) [1986] 2 All E.R. 488.

[47] *Supra*, n. 44.

[48] *Ibid.*

[49] Notably of Upjohn J. in *Re Herbert Wagg & Co.* [1956] Ch. 323 340.

[50] The exceptions to the principle that an express choice of law is conclusive of the intentions of the parties relate only to public policy issues, and not to contractual difficulties created by such a choice: see *supra*, n. 3.

Causation and Proof of Loss in Marine Insurance

PETER MUCHLINSKI

The issue of causation and proof of loss is central to marine insurance litigation. To succeed in his claim the assured must show that the loss of his insured interest was caused by an "insured peril," that is, by some cause of loss, the risk of which the insurer has accepted under the insurance contract. In doing so the assured must prove that, on a balance of probabilities, the loss was due to an insured peril. The underwriter may seek to avoid liability by arguing that no causal relation exists between the loss and an insured peril. He may do this in two related ways.

First he may argue that the cause of loss is not within the risk contemplated by the insurance, because it is excluded as a matter of general law and/or under the terms of the policy. In the latter case this may be due to an exclusion clause, or to a restriction of the kinds of losses covered by the policy in the risks clause. Further defences based on the absence of causal relation may arise where the policy runs off between successive causes of loss, or where it is necessary to determine, for the purposes of calculating an indemnity, whether two successive losses by insured perils should be treated as separate casualties.[1]

Secondly, the insurer may argue that the assured has failed to discharge his burden of proving that the loss was caused by an insured peril. This may be done by setting up an alternative, and equally plausible, explanation for the loss that falls outside the risk, or simply by showing that the evidence adduced by the assured fails to establish a prima facie case of loss by an insured peril.

It is the purpose of this paper to consider the implications of these defences, and to examine how the applicable doctrines have evolved in the field of marine insurance. Before this is done two general points should be made. First, the defences of the insurer arise from the nature of the contract of insurance as a contract of indemnity. Its purpose is to shift risk to the insurer, who, in theory, is the better risk taker. To achieve this the insurer must have a clear perception of the risk that he undertakes. His risk is laid down in the insurance contract and he will be liable only if the assured's loss falls within the contemplated risk.[2] There is, therefore, no room for broad principles of insurer's liability. The assured must show a clear causal connection between the loss suffered and an insured peril. Secondly, although the doctrine of causation appears in various branches of the law, it may not be possible to assimilate its application in marine insurance with a general theory of causation in the law. For, despite the use of common terms and the common objective of isolating, from a number of causally relevant facts, those causal facts that are of especial legal significance to the issue at hand, a unified doctrine of causation may not exist. Consequently, the doctrine of causation in marine insurance should be analysed within the framework of the substantive law of marine insurance, rather than as part of a general theory of causation in the law.

A. *The Doctrine of Causation in Marine Insurance*

1. *"Proximate Cause"*

The doctrine of causation acts as a test of insurer's liability under a marine policy. By section 55(1) of the Marine Insurance Act 1906:

> "Subject to the provisions of this Act, and unless the policy otherwise provides, the insurer is liable for any loss proximately caused by a peril insured against, but, subject as aforesaid, he is not liable for any loss which is not proximately caused by a peril insured against."

This provision stresses that "proximate cause" is the basis of the doctrine of causation in marine insurance. It also gives the parties the right to exclude the doctrine by contract. Such exclusion will, however, remain subject to review in the light of public policy, legality and contractual construction.[3]

Causa proxima non remota spectatur is regarded as a fundamental principle of marine insurance.[4] It is to be found among Bacon's *Maxims*. Bacon glosses the maxim by stating[5]:

> "it were infinite for the law to judge the causes of causes, and their impulsions one of another; therefore it contenteth it selfe with the immediate cause, and judgeth of acts by that without looking to any further degree."

According to Beale, Bacon is here attempting to show that the law is concerned only with the immediate physical cause of an event and, once that is established, it need not examine the chain of causation leading to the ultimate cause.[6] For legal purposes the ultimate cause may be irrelevant, as where the ultimate cause of a murder committed with a gun may be the manufacture of the weapon.

Bacon's maxim was applied by Blackburn J. in *Dudgeon v. Pembroke*.[7] In that case the insured vessel was lost by stranding, after having earlier taken in water in bad weather. The water could not be pumped out, as the pumps got choked with oats that had entered from the hold via a defective screw tunnel. The evidence showed that, on the outward voyage, more water was entering the vessel than could be accounted for by the weather. Furthermore, the vessel had been laid up for some eighteen months before being repaired and brought into service by the assured.

The insurers argued that the true cause of loss was the unseaworthiness of the ship and not a peril of the seas. Blackburn J. rejected this argument and, applying Bacon's maxim, held that the immediate cause of the loss was a peril of the seas.[8]

The Exchequer Chamber overturned this judgment by a majority,[9] holding that there was an implied warranty as to seaworthiness in a time policy, which applied at the commencement of the risk when, as in the present case, the assured was in actual control of the vessel. The vessel was found to be unseaworthy and, as the unseaworthiness was the true cause of the loss, the assured could not recover.

The House of Lords reversed this judgment.[10] The terms of a time policy did not admit an implied warranty of the kind described by the Exchequer Chamber. The insurer could only escape liability if he could show that the vessel was lost solely and immediately through the operation of its unseaworthiness. On the facts that was not possible, as the immediate cause of loss was the stranding and/or the heavy weather.

Dudgeon v. Pembroke offers a classic illustration of the "proximate" or "immediate" cause doctrine in action. What is particularly striking is the extent to which the issue turned on the construction of the contract. Had their Lordships held that the warranty of seaworthiness applies to time policies just as to voyage policies, the issue of causation would have been avoided altogether. The evidence of unseaworthiness would have given the insurer a good defence irrespective of any causal connection between it and the loss of the vessel. The case shows that questions of causation in marine insurance hang on the initial construction of the contract. As Lord Shaw noted in *Leyland Shipping Co. Ltd. v. Norwich Union Fire Ins. Soc. Ltd.*,[11] "the true and overriding principle is to look at a contract as a whole and ascertain what the parties to it really meant. What was it which brought about the loss, the event, the calamity, the accident? And this is not in an artificial sense, but in that real sense which parties to a contract must have had in their minds when they spoke of cause at all."

This stress on the contemplation of future risk by the parties has important effects on causal questions. We are dealing here not only with the actual physical causes of loss; rather, we are asking whether the loss that occurs ought to be indemnified given the limits that the insurer has placed on his risk. The proximate cause of the loss is determined in the light of this consideration.

This may be the reason why the courts have not developed any sophisticated theory of cause and effect and have preferred to take a pragmatic approach. In the words of Lord Dunedin in the *Leyland Shipping* case, "the case turns on a pure question of fact to be determined by common-sense principles,"[12] and the search is for, "the dominant cause of the loss."[13] In the same case, Lord Shaw gave an instructive explanation of the doctrine, which is worth quoting at length[14]:

"To treat *proxima causa* as the cause which is nearest in time is out of the question. Causes are spoken of as if they were as distinct from one another as beads in a row or links in a chain, but—if this metaphysical topic has to be referred to—it is not wholly so. The chain of causation is a handy expression, but the figure is inadequate. Causation is not a chain but a net. At each point influences, forces, events, precedent and simultaneous, meet; and the radiation from each point extends infinitely. At the point where these various influences meet it is for the judgment as upon a matter of fact to declare which of the causes thus joined at the point of effect was the proximate and which was the remote cause. . . . The cause which is truly proximate is that which is proximate in efficiency. That efficiency may have been preserved although other causes may have in the meantime sprung up which have not yet destroyed it, or truly impaired it, and it may culminate in a result of which it still remains the real efficient cause to which the event can be ascribed."

It is clear from this passage that the doctrine of proximate cause leaves much discretion to the judge of fact, especially if he is to be guided by "common-sense" principles.

It is also clear that the "proximate" or "immediate" cause is not the last event in time or space before the loss occurs. Nonetheless, the last event may be, and often is, regarded as the proximate cause. Thus in *Cory* v. *Burr*,[15] where the barratry of the master led to the capture and seizure of the vessel, the loss was imputed to the latter, final, cause even though it would not have happened but for the earlier barratry. Similarly, in *The Salem*[16] the assured was allowed to recover under a cargo policy, which converted a loss of goods by the scuttling of the ship in which they were being carried into a loss by perils of the seas, because the proximate cause of the loss was the sinking of the vessel, and not the earlier conspiracy by the shipowners to defraud the hull insurers.

In the former case, it would have flown in the face of the contract to have held that the true cause of loss was barratry, where the loss to the assured arose out of costs incurred in repossessing the ship from the authorities that had seized it. In the latter case, to have held that the conspiracy was the effective cause of loss would have been to ignore the special clause that protected the assured against the loss of his cargo by a scuttling to which he was not a party. The clause had been inserted because the insurance was not on "all risks" terms, and so would not have covered loss by scuttling in the absence of the clause. Furthermore, it was a provision designed to avoid the legal effects of the House of Lords decision in *P. Samuel & Co. Ltd.* v. *Dumas*,[17] which held that a loss by scuttling on the part of the shipowner was not a loss by perils of the seas under the policies taken out on the vessel or cargo by innocent third parties. Thus, there was a clear contractual intention to cover the loss that occurred, and the court was free to regard that loss as the proximate cause when, ordinarily, the law would have given the conspiracy to scuttle overriding causal force.

In each case, therefore, the courts interpreted the effective cause of loss not in terms of a "but for" test of causation, but in terms of the risk assumed by the insurer under the policy. In other cases, the same approach has led the court to identify a cause more remote in time as the effective cause of loss.

For example, in the *Leyland Shipping* case,[18] a ship was insured by a time policy against perils of the seas. The policy contained a warranty against all the consequences of hostilities, the policy having been taken out during the early stages of the First World War. In January 1915, the ship was torpedoed by a U-boat of the Germany Navy. The vessel was towed to Le Havre, where it was safely berthed. It was subsequently moved, on the orders of the port authorities, to an outer breakwater, a site subject to the ebb and flood of tides. The vessel broke up and sank under the action of the tides.

The House of Lords held that the torpedoing, and not the extra-ordinary action of the tides, was the proximate cause of loss and so the underwriters were protected by the warranty. The decision can be explained on the ground that, in wartime, many vessels would be hit by torpedoes but would not sink straight away. Nonetheless, they would be more at risk of loss by an insured peril after the attack, which would undoubtedly weaken the vessel's ability to withstand the wind and waves. This must have been in the contemplation of the insurers when inserting the warranty into the policy. Therefore, to hold that, where a torpedo damaged vessel is subsequently lost by the operation of an insured peril, the proximate cause of loss is the insured peril is to ignore the limits of the cover offered to the assured.

Sometimes the courts may be tempted to introduce policy considerations into their analysis of causation. This may explain why the courts at times come to different decisions on seemingly similar facts, and where an approach based on a strict interpretation of the contract suggests a single answer. The cases concerning measures taken to avert or minimise loss by insured perils illustrate the point. The basic issue of causation is whether there was an actual operation of an insured peril in relation to which such measures were taken.[19] The leading cases concern insurance on cargoes, or freight, where the subject-matter insured is lost through the termination of the marine adventure by the taking of measures to avoid an apprehended loss by capture and seizure.

The applicable principle was established in *Hadkinson* v. *Robinson*[20] as follows:

> "where underwriters have insured against capture and restraint of princes and the captain, learning that if he enters the port of his destination the vessel will be lost by confiscation, avoids the port, whereby the object of the voyage is defeated—such circumstances do not amount to a peril operating to the total destruction of the thing insured."

The assured could only abandon in respect of a loss of voyage where the loss was occasioned by an insured peril. That had to be a peril acting "immediately and not circuitously."

The House of Lords affirmed the principle of *Hadkinson* v. *Robinson* in *Becker, Gray & Co.* v. *London Assurance Corp.*[21] It was held that, where a British-owned cargo was carried in a German ship on a voyage to Germany, and the ship's captain decided to make for a neutral port in anticipation of capture by a British naval vessel, but where no actual chase had occurred, the cargo owners could not recover for loss by restraint of princes. The act of the master was a voluntary act not brought about by the immediate operation of an insured peril, and so was outside the cover. In the course of his speech, Lord Sumner stressed that the case involved nothing more nor less than giving effect to the "real meaning of the parties to a contract of insurance."[22] It was not a question of doing "the liberal and reasonable thing by a reasonable assured."[23] In other words, it would have been wrong to hold the underwriters liable in circumstances where it appeared that a loss outside the assumed risk had occurred.

However, in *British and Foreign Marine Ins. Co. Ltd.* v. *Samuel Sanday & Co.*,[24] the House of Lords had earlier rejected the underwriter's understanding of the limits of their risk, and had held them liable on facts not dissimilar to those in *Becker*'s case. In *Sanday*'s case, British cargo owners had insured goods being carried to Germany in British ships. During the voyage, the British Government declared war on Germany, making trading with the enemy illegal. The ships were directed to proceed to British ports. The cargo owners warehoused their goods and claimed for a constructive total loss. The House of Lords held that there was a restraint of princes within the policy. The declaration of war was the proximate cause of the loss for, once it had been made, the cargo owners and the shipowners had no alternative but to observe its consequences and to interrupt their voyages. To have continued would have amounted to a breach of the law, which prohibited trading with the enemy.

According to the editors of *Arnould*, the decision in *Sanday*'s case, "came as a surprise to underwriters, involving them in a risk of a political nature which they had hardly contemplated."[25] In this case, the assured appeared to have been given the benefit of the doubt, perhaps because the House of Lords felt that British subjects should be encouraged to obey the law regarding trading with the enemy, by ensuring that they would receive compensation for so doing.

If that were so, then why did the British cargo owners in *Becker*'s case not succeed? *Sanday*'s case was there distinguished on the ground that the German captain was free to disobey the British blockade, and his decision to make for a neutral port was voluntary. Its voluntary character could not be destroyed by the fact that the British cargo owners were bound not to trade with the enemy. It may be that the House of Lords in *Becker* had taken the contractual limits of the insurer's risk more seriously than in *Sanday*'s case, where the duties of the subject to the sovereign seemed to be the determining factor.

The insurer's displeasure with *Sanday*'s case was subsequently highlighted when the Institute of London Underwriters issued the "frustration clause" to exclude the operation of that case.[26] The lesson seems to be that, if the courts will not accept the limits of insurer's risk as stated in the policy and commonly understood in practice and interpret issues as to proximate cause in accordance with that standard, the insurers will exclude the operation of the court's decisions.

It is convenient to remain with the interpretation of the "frustration clause" to consider a further important issue of causation: whether the loss is caused by an insured peril or is due to an excepted peril. Certain cases, such as *Atlantic Maritime Co. Inc.* v. *Gibbon*,[27] have approached the problem by applying the immediate cause doctrine. Following the reasoning in *Cory* v. *Burr*,[28] the Court of Appeal held that the loss to the assured, arising out of the abandonment of a voyage due to an immediate peril of loss by restraint of princes and warlike operations, was a loss covered by the "frustration clause."

Cory v. *Burr* and *Atlantic Maritime Co. Inc.* v. *Gibbon* both apply the immediate cause rule to cases involving a succession of losses, the last of which is an expected peril. More difficult are cases of concurrent causes of loss one of which is an excepted peril. Again the question depends on the construction of the contract and, in particular, on the construction of the exclusion clause. However, there is authority for the view that cases of concurrent loss involving the operation of an excluded peril are subject to a conclusive presumption that the excluded peril is the proximate cause of loss. Thus, in the opinion of the editors of *Arnould*, it is, "virtually beyond doubt, that there can be no recovery where there are two causes of loss, each of which is capable of being regarded as the proximate cause, and one of which is an excepted peril."[29] They base their opinion on a public liability insurance case, *Wayne Tank & Pump Co. Ltd.* v. *Employer's Liability Assurance Corp. Ltd.*[30]

In that case, the assured were engineers who designed and installed equipment for storing and conveying liquid wax in a factory making plasticine. They had a policy indemnifying them against all damages which they became liable to pay as a result of accidents, happening in the course of their business, and causing damage on premises described in the policy. These included the plasticine factory. The policy was subject to an exception with respect to "damage caused by the nature or condition of any goods . . . sold or supplied by or on behalf of the insured." The factory subsequently burned down, partly as a result of dangerously defective equipment installed by the assured and partly as the result of the conduct of an employee, who had left the installation switched on and unattended overnight before it had been tested. At first instance, Mocatta J. held that the assured could recover under the policy. The Court of Appeal reversed that decision on grounds of causation.

Lord Denning M.R. and Roskill L.J. held that the dominant and effective cause of the loss was the nature of the goods supplied. Thus, the loss was caused by an excepted peril. Their Lordships added that, if there was not one dominant cause, but two causes which were equal or nearly equal in bringing about the loss, and one of them was within an exception to liability, the insurers could rely on the exception clause. Roskill L.J. concluded that[31]:

> "the law in this respect is the same both for marine and non-marine, namely, that if the loss is caused by two causes effectively operating at the same time and one is wholly expressly excluded from the policy, the policy does not pay."

Cairns L.J. was, by contrast, not prepared to find a single effective cause of loss. He believed that the court should not strain to find a dominant cause if, as in the present case, there were two causes both of which could be described as the effective causes of loss. In such cases the insurer was saved from liability by the exception.[32] Cairns L.J. was the only judge in the case who based his decision on this principle. Lord Denning M.R. and Roskill L.J. accepted it only *obiter*, having held that the excepted peril was the sole proximate cause of the loss.

The authority cited by their Lordships for the existence of the alleged principle appears weak. Lord Denning M.R. was content to rest the matter on a rule of contractual construction,[33] while Roskill L.J. based his view on an implication from *obiter dicta* in *Cory* v. *Burr*,[34] an argument of leading counsel in the *Leyland Shipping* case,[35] and a dictum from the dissenting speech of Lord Sumner in *Samuel* v. *Dumas*.[36] There is not one *ratio* of a decided case quoted in favour of the rule.

The proposed principle may be doubted on further grounds. First, it begs the question of causation to assume that the excepted peril must be the effective cause of loss. Secondly, a full inquiry into the cause of loss is required if justice to the assured is to be done. Thirdly, it places too great an evidential burden on the assured, who must show that there was a loss by an insured peril and convince the court that there was no concurrent operation of an excepted peril. All the insurer need do is to show that another, excepted, peril may have contributed to the loss. Whether it actually did so is no longer the question. Fourthly, the effect of an

exclusion clause in a contract of insurance should not be determined by general rules of law. The scope of the clause must be
gathered from its own terms, and not every exclusion clause will
operate in the manner suggested by the general rule.

For example, in *The Miss Jay Jay*,[37] a time policy on a vessel
owned by the assured excluded recovery for loss or expenditure
incurred, *inter alia*, solely in the event of damage resulting from
faulty design, or in the event of the replacement or repair of any
part condemned solely in consequence of a latent defect or fault or
error in design and construction. The vessel was damaged in a
rough sea in circumstances where a better designed and con-
structed vessel of the same class should not have experienced difficulties. The assured went to considerable expense to repair the
vessel and claimed under the policy. The insurers sought to rely on
the exclusion clause. Mustill J. rejected this contention, and his
decision was upheld by the Court of Appeal.

On its true construction the exclusion operated only where
defects in design and manufacture were the sole cause of the
expenditure. In the present case there was an intervening peril, the
rough weather, which, given the condition of the vessel, amounted
to a peril of the seas that was within the policy cover. Although the
defect in the vessel and the rough seas apparently operated simul-
taneously to cause the loss (and, indeed, the loss may only have
been caused by the combination of both causes), the exclusion
clause demanded that the defect in design had to be the sole cause
of loss in order that the insurer could benefit from it.

Thus, the scope of an exclusion clause depends on its terms, and
not every such clause will admit the approach suggested by the editors of *Arnould* on the basis of dicta in the *Wayne Tank* case. It
appears from the judgment of the Court of Appeal in *The Miss Jay
Jay* that a distinction must be made between cases where a concurrent cause of loss is expressly excluded by the policy, and those
where the policy limits the exclusion to circumstances in which the
excluded peril is the sole effective cause of loss. The principle suggested by the Court of Appeal in the *Wayne Tank* case applies to
the former situation alone. The message to insurers seems to be to
draft exclusion clauses that do not depend for their effect upon a
finding that the excluded peril was *the* effective cause of loss, but
to make them capable of covering cases where the excluded peril
was *a* concurrent and effective cause of loss. Thus, according to
Slade L.J., had there been a relevant express exclusion clause
relating to loss caused by the unseaworthiness of the vessel, the
plaintiff's claim in *The Miss Jay Jay* might well have been unsustainable.

This opinion is disturbing in view of the fact that the plaintiff was a private boat owner who might not have had the means of knowing that the vessel was unseaworthy. Nor could such a person be expected to understand the distinction between broad and narrow exclusion clauses made by the Court of Appeal, which, in practice, would appear as a rather subtle change in the wording of the exclusion clause in a standard form policy. It is to be hoped that in future cases like *The Miss Jay Jay*, but where a broader exclusion of liability for unseaworthiness exists, the courts will protect the assured by not sidestepping the issue of causation through the use of a presumption that the mere existence, on the facts, of an excluded peril alongside an insured peril relieves the insurer from liability. It must be remembered that we are dealing not with promissory warranties that must be strictly observed by the assured, but with exceptive warranties that limit the insurer's liability. Consequently, the interests of both parties must be taken into account when such a clause is in issue, and the courts should not give to the insurer the benefit of any doubt. They are bound to determine whether the insured and the excluded causes of loss are equally effective or not. That is quite clearly demanded by the actual decision in the *Wayne Tank* case.

To summarise: the proximate cause doctrine is applied in marine insurance as a means of ensuring that the assumption of risk by the insurer, as shown by the terms of the insurance contract, is not upset by allowing claims that have no causal connection with the risks undertaken by the insurer. In this process the courts are bound to interpret the contract in order to ascertain, first, whether any problem of causation arises on the terms of the contract in the light of the facts of the case and, secondly, if it does, to determine which of the various causes of loss put forward to explain the casualty is the legally relevant cause. In answering these questions the courts have assumed "common-sense" notions of causation.[38] In practice this means that the courts exercise a considerable measure of discretion in interpreting whether a proximate cause question arises, and in choosing between different causes as the dominant or effective cause. In so doing they run the risk of confusing policy issues with issues of causation, as the question of causation may raise the broader issue of whether, as a matter of justice, the assured ought to recover or whether the insurer ought to avoid liability. In giving answers to questions of causation the courts have undoubtedly borne such considerations in mind. In certain commonly met cases of loss the court's answers to these questions have evolved into principles concerning the limits of insurers' liability, displaying the particular concerns of justice in this field. To these we now turn.

2. *The limits of insurers' liability*

Certain limits to insurers' liability are well settled in law. They are reproduced in section 55(2) of the Marine Insurance Act 1906 as follows:

"(a) the insurer is not liable for any loss attributable to the wilful misconduct of the assured, but, unless the policy otherwise provides, he is liable for any loss proximately caused by a peril insured against, even though the loss would not have happened but for the misconduct or negligence of the master and crew;

(b) Unless the policy otherwise provides, the insurer on ship or goods is not liable for any loss proximately caused by delay, although the delay may be caused by a peril insured against;

(c) Unless the policy otherwise provides, the insurer is not liable for ordinary wear and tear, ordinary leakage and breakage, inherent vice or nature of the subject-matter insured, or for any loss proximately caused by rats or vermin, or for any injury to machinery not proximately caused by maritime perils."

It is not proposed to consider the law relating to each limitation in detail.[39] The purpose of this section is to explain, in terms of the doctrine of causation, the role of the limits to liability set out in section 55(2). In this respect, particular attention will be paid to the limitations in section 55(2)(a), as these raise some of the most difficult conceptual issues and so afford the best material for study.

The starting point is the nature of the loss that is insured against under a marine policy. Such a loss will be foreseeable only in the general sense that losses of the kind covered are likely to occur as an incident of maritime adventures. It must, above all, be fortuitous: it must involve an element of "accident or casualty." In *British and Foreign Marine Insurance Co.* v. *Gaunt*,[40] a case involving an "all risks" policy on goods, Lord Sumner described certain general principles of causation on which the limits of insurer's liability have been worked out. First, the loss cannot be caused by the ordinary action of the environment on the subject-matter insured. Such loss by ordinary wear and tear is inevitable, and insurance against normal depreciation is not usual in the absence of express provision in the policy. Secondly, deterioration due to the inherent nature of the subject-matter insured cannot be the cause of loss. Again, this is inevitable and cannot be covered without special provision.[41] Thirdly, where the assured is in some way to blame for the loss, it ought not to be recoverable. To hold otherwise might encourage avoidable carelessness, if not the deliberate destruction of the subject-matter insured. However, as will be seen below, this general principle is subject to qualification in cases where negligence of the assured or of the master and crew brings about a loss by an insured peril. All these cases can be subsumed in the general principle that losses that are inevitable rather than fortuitous cannot be the subject of a marine insurance claim.

The limits to insurers' liability in section 55(2) are all, with the exception of wilful misconduct of the assured, subject to modification by contract. The parties are free to extend cover to otherwise excluded perils. Wilful misconduct of the assured is excluded from this freedom on grounds of policy, as it might involve the criminal destruction of property and insurance fraud.[42]

Given this attitude to the wilful misconduct of the assured, it may be surprising, in terms of the requirement of fortuitous loss, to find that the law accepts loss caused by the negligence of the assured as a loss proximately caused by an insured peril, where the act of negligence leads directly to a loss by an insured peril.[43] Similarly, the negligence of the master and crew, so long as it constitutes an effective cause of loss by an insured peril, is no bar to recovery.[44] Only where negligence is expressly excluded from the policy, or is such that the insurer has a defence under section 39(5)[45] or section 78(4)[46] of the Marine Insurance Act 1906, will it prevent the assured from recovering.

The justification for this treatment of negligence was recently considered by the Supreme Court of Canada in *Century Insurance Co. of Canada* v. *Case Existological Laboratories Ltd., (The Bamcell II)*.[47] In that case, the insured vessel sank when an employee of the assured negligently left open some valves, thereby allowing water to enter the craft's compartments. The assured claimed for a loss by perils of the seas. At first instance, McKenzie J. held that the loss was not a loss by "perils of the seas" on the ground that, once the valve had been opened, and remained open, it was inevitable that the vessel would sink. There was no "fortuitous accident." The Court of Appeal reversed the decision by a majority. The Supreme Court accepted the majority opinion and adopted the following passage from the judgment of Lambert J.A. in the Court of Appeal[48]:

"An act is not negligent in itself but only in relation to a foreseeable risk of harm. If that foreseeable risk of harm is peculiarly a marine risk, then the act, coupled with its foreseeable consequence, is a fortuitous accident of the seas and a peril of the seas and proximate cause of loss."

This decision has been criticised on the ground that it is based on doubtful authority, and that it draws the risk undertaken by the insurer too widely.[49] The major problem is whether it is possible for a "foreseeable risk of harm" to constitute a "fortuitous accident." The degree of foresight involved must be quite low for the element of fortuitousness to survive. Otherwise the assured could recover for losses that were a highly probable result of his negligence (or that of the master and crew). It would make the fact of negligence itself a ground of recovery. In the absence of special provision to this effect in the policy, such a result cannot be admitted, as it would permit recovery for a certainty, not a risk. Even where negligence creates an increased risk of loss, and can be causally connected to the loss on a "but for" test, the loss must be sufficiently unforeseeable to be accidental.

It is in this sense that one should read the reference by Lord Wright in *Canada Rice Mills Ltd.* v. *Union Marine and General Insurance Co.*,[50] to some negligent act, causing accidental incursion of sea water, as an example of loss by perils of the seas. The Supreme Court of Canada in *The Bamcell II* seems to have taken this reference to imply a broader principle, which makes the insurer's liability depend on a concept of foresight that is more appropriate to establishing liability in the law of tort than to limiting insurer's liability in marine insurance. Furthermore, unless a clear distinction is maintained between "foreseeable" and "fortuitous" loss occasioned by negligent acts, it could make recovery easier for what is, in effect, wilful misconduct. This distinction will become harder to draw if the decision of the Supreme Court of Canada is followed.

By contrast with negligence, the wilful misconduct of the assured, or of the master and crew, cannot be regarded as a fortuitous cause of loss.[51] Consequently, the assured cannot recover where the misconduct is the proximate cause of loss. Indeed, in the case of wilful misconduct by the assured, recovery is barred even where the misconduct is a remote cause of loss. In the words of section 55(2)(a), the loss need be only "attributable" to the misconduct. Similarly, in the case of wilful misconduct by the master and crew, in the absence of a term to the contrary, the insurer is only liable where the misconduct is the remote cause of a loss by an insured peril.

This may cause hardship to the innocent assured, such as an innocent cargo owner whose cargo has been lost when the vessel in which it was being carried is scuttled. The cargo owner may protect himself either by taking out an "all risks" policy under the Institute Cargo Clauses (A) or by adding the Institute Malicious Damage Clause[52] to the (B) and (C) Clauses, if these form the basis of the policy. In this way, the assured remains covered even where the wilful misconduct of third parties is the proximate cause of loss.

The preceding discussion has highlighted the relationship between the nature and cause of loss in marine insurance. Again, the issue turns on what the insurer has accepted as the limit of his risk. The cases covered by section 55(2) of the Marine Insurance Act 1906 stress the fortuitous nature of the proximate cause of loss as a general condition of recovery, subject to contractual variation, save in the case of wilful misconduct of the assured, where the insurer is protected even where the misconduct is a remote cause of loss.

3. Conclusion

The doctrine of causation in marine insurance is a means of limiting the insurer's liability to cases of fortuitous loss, coming strictly within the terms of the cover. This minimum of liability can be increased by the terms of the insurance, but this is strictly a matter of agreement between the parties. The courts have not, in general, intervened on the side of the assured, save where the cover clearly extends to the loss or for particular reasons of policy. The latter case appears, however, to be rare. Indeed, the policy of the law may be to favour the insurer in cases of doubt. With this in mind, attention will now turn to the insurer's defence of holding the assured to proof on the issue of causation.

B. *Proof of Loss in Marine Insurance*

1. *The general burden and standard of proof*

The assured has the onus of proving that, on a balance of probabilities, the loss was caused by an insured peril.[53] The discharge of this requirement varies with the extent of the cover.[54] The more limited the cover, the greater the burden on the assured to prove the specific cause of loss. For example, in an insurance on war risks alone, the court must be "satisfied beyond reasonable doubt" that the subject matter insured is lost as a result of a war risk.[55] This should not be taken to mean that the criminal standard of proof applies, but it certainly requires proof of a high probability of loss by an insured peril.

In policies against marine risks the assured must first make out a prima facie case of loss by an insured peril. The level of proof required to make out a prima facie case varies according to the circumstances of the loss and the extent of cover under the policy.

Thus, where a ship sails out of port and is never heard of again, there is a presumption of loss by a peril of the seas with all hands.[56] However, if there is evidence as to the cause of the sinking, as where there are survivors, then the assured may not be entitled to this presumption and may be held to full proof.[57] The policy may influence the degree of proof required, by the manner in which the risk is described. Thus, a distinction must be made between exceptions that qualify the whole of the insurer's promise to indemnify and those that only partly qualify it. In the former case, the assured would have to show not only that the loss was prima facie caused by an insured peril but also that it fell outside the general exception. In the latter case only a prima facie case of loss need be established to shift the evidential burden.[58]

When the assured has made out a prima facie case of loss by an insured peril, the insurer may defend either by holding the assured to the strict burden of proof or by setting up an alternative explanation of the loss that falls outside the cover.

According to Lord Evershed M.R., the underwriter is always entitled to require strict proof of the cause of loss.[59] Otherwise the assured would be able to succeed without discharging the onus of proof, especially where the insurer has given no notice of any alternative explanation of the loss in his pleadings, which would bar him from introducing such a defence at the trial.

Should the insurer wish to set up an alternative explanation of the loss, he too may enjoy certain presumptions in his favour. In particular, he may allege that the vessel was lost through unseaworthiness where it sinks in good weather soon after leaving port.[60] He will do this where the assured relies on the loss itself as evidence of loss by an unascertained peril of the seas. It shifts the burden back onto the assured to show that the ship was seaworthy. If he fails to do so the inference is that the ship was not lost by an insured peril. To succeed, the assured must show that the vessel was seaworthy at the commencement of the voyage.[61]

This differs from the case where the assured can make out a prima facie case of loss by insured peril. It is then up to the insurer to set up a prima facie case of loss by unseaworthiness in order to rely on the implied warranty of seaworthiness in a voyage policy or, in the case of a time policy, to raise the question whether the loss was caused by unseaworthiness. It is then up to the assured to show, on a balance of probabilities, that the proximate cause of the loss was an insured peril. He need not disprove unseaworthiness where a time policy is involved, as this is irrelevant to the insurer's liability if it is not the effective cause of loss.[62]

In certain cases the evidence as to competing causes of loss may be evenly balanced, and it may be doubtful whether the loss is attributable to an insured or excluded peril. This was the problem facing the courts in *Rhesa Shipping Co. S.A.* v. *Edmunds (The Popi M)*.[63] In that case, the vessel sank due to an unexplained entry of sea-water into her engine room through a hole in the shell plating. This occurred in good weather and calm seas off the coast of Algeria. It appeared that, but for the negligence of the crew in failing to carry out properly repairs to the bilge pump valves, the vessel would not have sunk. The owners claimed under time policies for loss by perils of the seas or, alternatively, by negligence of the crew. The underwriters denied liability, claiming that the loss was caused by the decayed condition of the ship or, if it was due to crew negligence, it fell within the due diligence exception in the Institute Time Clauses.

At first instance,[64] Bingham J. held that the negligence issue was part of the broader issue of unseaworthiness, and the case proceeded on that basis. On the evidence, his Lordship could not conclude that the vessel was seaworthy on the day she sank. Equally, the underwriters could not show that the vessel was unseaworthy. Regarding the cause of loss, the assured suggested that the hole in the side of the vessel must have been made through contact with a submerged object such as a submarine. The underwriters adduced expert evidence to substantiate the wear and tear hypothesis but Bingham J. felt that it could not support this theory of the cause of loss. In these circumstances he felt free to accept the improbable explanation of the assured, as any other explanation was effectively ruled out.

The decision of Bingham J. was upheld by the Court of Appeal,[65] although May L.J. felt that the judge had erred in holding that the assured had met the burden of proof. The House of Lords reversed the decision of both of the lower courts.[66] Citing Scrutton L.J. in *Martiartu* v. *Royal Exchange Assurance Corp.*,[67] their Lordships held that it was always open to the court to conclude that the proximate cause of loss remains in doubt and that the shipowners have failed to discharge the burden of proof. Bingham J. was wrong to accept such an improbable explanation of the loss simply because no better explanation was forthcoming. Lord Brandon, delivering the judgment of the House, concluded that the legal concept of proof of a cause on a balance of probabilities had to be applied with common-sense and that Bingham J.'s finding did not accord with common-sense.[68]

It would appear from this decision that, where the assured cannot explain the cause of loss on a strict balance of probabilities, the insurer need not go to the trouble of showing an alternative cause of loss and can simply hold the assured to proof in order to succeed.

This case clearly favours the insurer. There must be clear proof of loss by an insured peril before the assured can recover. It may be thought that this operates too harshly against the assured, in that it relieves the insurer of the burden of proving, on a balance of probabilities, that the loss was a loss by excepted perils. It may be that Bingham J., in coming to his decision, did not wish to allow the insurers such an evidential advantage, and so gave the assured the benefit of the doubt.

In terms of the principle of indemnity the decision of the House of Lords must be correct. The insurer ought not to pay where the conditions of payment set out in the insurance are not proved. However, this may give the insurer too easy an opportunity to avoid liability. All he requires, it seems, is a client who owns an old vessel that is difficult to keep in a state of perfect repair, to have the necessary evidence to cast doubt on the assured's case. If subsequent cases interpret *The Popi M* in this way they may be going too far.

However, in one area of disputes over causation this may be precisely the approach that is required. That area involves cases where the shipowner alleges loss by an insured peril and the insurer introduces evidence of scuttling.

2. *The burden and standard of proof in cases of alleged scuttling*

In this situation, it may be desirable to give the insurer the benefit of the doubt. The assured should not be allowed to win his case on equivocal evidence, in case he has in fact deliberately cast the vessel away. The discussion of this issue has centred on the degree of proof required of the insurer to establish scuttling as the cause of loss.

The case law in this area is unsettled. There are cases in which it has been held that the civil standard of proof applies,[69] and others in which the insurer has been held to the criminal standard of "proof beyond reasonable doubt."[70] This is justified on the ground that an allegation of scuttling involves an allegation of criminal conduct, and so the presumption of innocence must be observed.

A number of writers feel that the civil standard of proof should remain the applicable standard in cases of scuttling.[71] They argue that no issue of the guilt or innocence of the assured arises in such cases. The assured must make out a prima facie case of loss by an insured peril. The inclusion of a presumption of innocence would mean that he would no longer have to show that the vessel was cast away without his privity, and it would place a heavy burden on the insurer to prove such privity "beyond reasonable doubt." In effect, the assured would succeed by simply alleging the barratry of the crew.

The views of the abovementioned writers concern the establishment of a prima facie case by the assured. Once he discharges this burden, and the insurer then raises the defence of loss by scuttling, the issue of which standard of proof has to be met remains. According to Branson J. in *The Gloria*[72]:

> "Scuttling is a crime and the court will not find that it has been committed unless it is proved with the same degree of certainty as is required for the proof of a crime."

The editors of *Arnould* do not believe that this statement means that the criminal standard of proof applies. However, the standard of proof is, they feel, a higher one than would apply to a less serious allegation. "The allegation of wilful misconduct must, therefore, be proved on a clear balance of probability if the defence is to succeed."[73]

This view is in keeping with the general principle that "an allegation of criminal conduct . . . need be established only on a preponderance of probability in a civil action."[74] However, the matter may be nothing more than a linguistic issue. In practice, a serious allegation will require a higher degree of probability for its proof, and whether one calls this a "clear balance of probability" or "proof beyond reasonable doubt" may not matter very much. A civil court must be very careful before making an affirmative finding of loss by scuttling, in view of the serious commercial and legal consequences that may befall the assured once such a finding is made known. Therefore, once the assured has made out a prima facie case of loss by an insured peril, and the onus shifts to the insurer, the latter's standard of proof must be a high one, higher than if he alleged loss by any other excepted cause.

3. Conclusion

Cases of alleged scuttling provide the source of the requirement that the assured be kept strictly to proof and that, should the court remain in doubt as to whether a loss is caused by an insured or excepted peril, the assured must fail. The justification for such a strict approach in cases of scuttling is, no doubt, to hinder the success of the scuttler's fraud. The decision in *The Popi M* extends this principle to cases involving allegations of unseaworthiness. The principle appears to be becoming a general rule of marine insurance law. It is in keeping with a strict interpretation of insurer's liability but, if not used with restraint, it could become a cause of harshness against the assured.

C. *Conclusion*

This paper has examined the doctrines of causation and proof of loss in marine insurance as defences against claims of loss by an insured peril. In this they are analogous to other doctrines, such as non-disclosure and warranties, that seek to limit the insurer's liability only to losses that are within the initial assumption of risk.

The tendency in each of the doctrines under study is to give the insurer the benefit of the doubt. Otherwise, the assured could recover in circumstances not contemplated by the insurer. Where the courts appear to have done this, insurers have retorted by revising the available terms of insurance, thereby emphasising the fact that a contract of marine insurance is, ultimately, the insurer's contract.

In certain cases concerning causation and proof of loss, the courts display a tendency to go a long way in protecting insurers from liability, at times possibly too far. The field of marine insurance is deemed to be a field of genuine bargaining equality, and so to be outside the scope of the legal control of exclusions of liability.[75] Nevertheless, it is to be hoped that the courts will read such contracts with the expectations of both parties in mind and decide issues of causation and proof of loss accordingly.

Notes

[1] Arnould, *Law of Marine Insurance and Average* (16th ed., 1981), (hereafter cited as Arnould), para. 773. See too *Fooks* v. *Smith* [1924] 2 K.B. 508.

[2] See *Becker Gray & Co.* v. *London Assurance Co.* [1918] A.C. 101, 113, *per* Lord Sumner.

[3] See, *e.g. Overseas Commodities* v. *Style* [1958] 1 Lloyd's Rep. 546, 560; Institute Cargo Clauses 1982 (B) and (C), cl. 1.1 which lists risks in respect of which the test of proximate cause is not required.

[4] *Arnould*, para. 761.

[5] Bacon, *The Common Laws of England* Tract One "Maxims of the law" Rule 1, (London 1630).

[6] Beale, *The Proximate Consequences of an Act* (1920) 23 Harv.L.R. 633 at p. 634.

[7] (1874) L.R. 9 Q.B. 581.

[8] *Ibid.* at p. 595.

[9] (1876) 1 Q.B.D. 96.

[10] (1877) 2 App.Cas. 284.

[11] [1918] A.C. 350 at p. 369.

[12] *Ibid.* at p. 362.

[13] *Ibid.* at p. 363.

[14] *Ibid.* at p. 369.

[15] (1883) 8 App.Cas. 393.

[16] *Shell International Petroleum Co.* v. *Gibbs, The Salem* [1983] 2 A.C. 375 (H.L.).

[17] [1924] A.C. 431.

[18] *Supra*, n. 11.

[19] *Arnould, op. cit.*, para. 766.

[20] (1803) 3 B. & P. 388.

[21] [1918] A.C. 101.

[22] *Ibid.* at p. 112.

[23] *Ibid.* at p. 113.

[24] [1916] 1 A.C. 650.

[25] *Op. cit.* para. 891.

[26] See the 1982 Institute War Clauses (Cargo), cl. 3.7: "In no case shall this insurance cover . . . any claim based upon loss of or frustration of the voyage or adventure."

[27] [1954] 1 Q.B. 88 (C.A.).

[28] *Supra*, n. 15.

[29] *Op. cit.*, para. 777.

[30] [1974] Q.B. 57 (C.A.).

[31] *Ibid.* at p. 75.

[32] *Ibid.* at p. 69.

[33] That "general words always have to give way to particular provisions": *ibid* at p. 67.

[34] *Supra*, n. 15, especially at pp. 399–401, *per* Lord Blackburn.

[35] [1918] A.C. 350 at p. 352, *per* Mr Wright (later Lord Wright).

[36] [1924] A.C. 431 at p. 467.

[37] *J.J. Lloyd Instruments Ltd.* v. *Northern Star Insurance Co. Ltd. (The Miss Jay Jay)* [1985] 1 Lloyds Rep. 264; *affmd.* [1987] 1 Lloyd's Rep. 32; [1987] 1 L.M.C.L.Q. 22.

[38] On "common-sense" approaches to causation, see H. L. A. Hart and Tony Honore, *Causation in the Law* (2nd ed., 1985), Chap. 2.

[39] See *Arnould, op.cit.*, paras. 779–786.

[40] [1921] A.C. 41 at p. 57.

[41] See further Clarke, *Insurance Law: Recent Causes* [1983] 4 L.M.C.L.Q. 576 at 580–583.

[42] See *Arnould, op. cit.*, para. 786, n. 30 and authorities cited therein.

[43] See *Trinder Anderson and Co.* v. *Thames and Mersey Marine Ins. Co.* [1898] 2 Q.B. 114 (C.A.).

[44] This is expressly provided for by s.55(2)(a) of the Marine Insurance Act 1906.

[45] Sending an unseaworthy ship out to sea under a time policy with the privity of the assured.

[46] Failure to take reasonable measures to avert or minimise loss by an insured peril.

⁴⁷ (1984) 150 D.L.R. (3d) 9; [1984] 1 W.W.R. 97.

⁴⁸ (1982) 133 D.L.R. (3d) 727, at p. 735.

⁴⁹ See McEwen and McEwen [1984] 4 L.M.C.L.Q. 671.

⁵⁰ [1941] A.C. 55 at pp. 68–69.

⁵¹ See *Samuel* v. *Dumas* [1924] A.C. 431 at p. 453, *per* Viscount Finlay.

⁵² The 1982 Institute Malicious Damage Clause reads: "In consideration of an additional premium, it is hereby agreed that the exclusion 'deliberate damage to or deliberate destruction of the subject-matter insured or any part thereof by the wrongful act of any person or persons' is deemed to be deleted and further that this insurance covers loss of or damage to the subject-matter insured caused by malicious acts vandalism or sabotage subject always to the other exclusions contained in this insurance."

⁵³ *Rhesa Shipping Co. S.A.* v. *Edmunds (The Popi M)* [1985] 1 W.L.R. 948 at p. 951, *per* Lord Brandon.

⁵⁴ See *British and Foreign Marine Insurance Co. Ltd.* v. *Gaunt* [1921] A.C.41 at p. 58, *per* Lord Sumner.

⁵⁵ *Munro Brice & Co.* v. *War Risks Assn. Ltd.* [1918] 2 K.B. 78 at p. 80, *per* Bailhache J.

⁵⁶ *Green* v. *Brown* (1744) 2 Stra. 1199.

⁵⁷ *La Compania Martiartu* v. *Royal Exchange Assurance* [1923] 1 K.B. 650 at p. 657, *per* Scrutton L.J.

⁵⁸ *Munro Brice & Co.* v. *War Risks Assoc. Ltd. supra*, 88–89.

⁵⁹ *Regina Fur Co. Ltd.* v. *Bossom* [1958] 2 Lloyd's Rep. 425 at p. 428.

⁶⁰ *Skandia Insurance Co. Ltd.* v. *Skoljarev* (1979) 142 C.L.R. 375 (H.C.A.).

⁶¹ *Ibid.*

⁶² See *Dudgeon* v. *Pembroke, supra.*

⁶³ [1985] 1 W.L.R. 948 (H.L.).

⁶⁴ [1983] 2 Lloyds Rep. 235.

⁶⁵ [1984] 2 Lloyds Rep. 555.

⁶⁶ *Supra*, n. 63.

⁶⁷ *Supra*, n. 57.

⁶⁸ [1985] 1 W.L.R. at p. 956.

⁶⁹ See, *e.g. Compania Martiartu* v. *Royal Exchange Assurance Corp.*, *supra*, n. 57; *Piermay Shipping Co. S.A.* v. *Chester (The Michael)* [1979] 1 Lloyds Rep. 55 (Kerr J.), not supported on this point by the Court of Appeal: [1979] 2 Lloyds Rep. 1.

⁷⁰ *Elfie A. Issaios* v. *Marine Insurance Co.* (1923) 15 Ll.L.R. 186 (C.A.).

⁷¹ Hazelwood, *Barratry—the Scuttlers Easy Route to the Golden Prize* [1982] L.M.C.L.Q. 383. This is a valuable paper setting down the case for applying the civil standard of proof. Hazelwood's position receives general support from the editors of *Arnould*, *op. cit.*, at para. 1357.

⁷² *Compania Naviera Vascongada* v. *British and Foreign Marine Ins. Co. (The Gloria)* (1936) 54 Ll.L.R. 35 at p. 50.

⁷³ *Op. cit.*, para. 1358.

⁷⁴ *Cross on Evidence* (6th ed., 1985), at p. 148.

⁷⁵ See Law Commission Report No. 104: *Insurance Law: Non-disclosure and Breach of Warranty*, Cmnd. 8064 (1980), paras. 2.8–2.16. The view expressed in the text may be too wide. There are, according to the Law Commission, numerous instances of persons who are quite inexperienced in marine insurance taking out marine insurance policies, *e.g.* pleasure boat owners. Thus, even in this field, some measure of control over exclusions of liability may be required.

INDEX